Kanyadaan

VIJAY TENDULKAR (1928–2008) was a leading Indian playwright, movie and television writer, literary essayist, political journalist, and social commentator. He has more than fifty publications to his credit. Several of his plays have become Marathi theatre classics, and have been translated and performed in many Indian languages. Recipient of numerous prestigious awards such as the Padma Bhushan, the Vishnudas Bhave Memorial Award, and the Katha Chudamani Award, for successfully raising social issues through his plays, Tendulkar was one of the greatest playwrights of our times.

GOWRI RAMNARAYAN is a journalist and writer, with a Ph.D. in Aesthetics. She has also translated Tendulkar's *A Friend's Story* (*Mitrachi Ghosha*) (OUP 2001).

Kanyadaan

Vijay Tendulkar

Translated by
Gowri Ramnarayan

OXFORD
UNIVERSITY PRESS

OXFORD
UNIVERSITY PRESS

Oxford University Press is a department of the University of Oxford.
It furthers the University's objective of excellence in research, scholarship,
and education by publishing worldwide. Oxford is a registered trademark of
Oxford University Press in the UK and in certain other countries

Published in India by
Oxford University Press
22 Workspace, 2nd Floor, 1/22 Asaf Ali Road, New Delhi 110002, India

This English translation
© Oxford University Press 1996

The moral rights of the authors have been asserted

First Edition published in 1996
Oxford India Paperbacks 2002
31st impression 2022

Digitally Printed in 2025

ISBN-13: 978-0-19-566380-8
ISBN-10: 0-19-566380-2

Typeset by Excellent Laser Typesetters, Pitampura, Delhi 110 034
Printed in India by Manipal Technologies Limited, Manipal

Translator's Acknowledgements

I wish to acknowledge my gratitude to the following persons who helped me with this translation:

* Dr S. Subramanian (Vishnupriya) for his thorough inspection of the first draft.

* Vijay Tendulkar for his meticulous checking of the final version.

* Dr M. Sivaramakrishna, once Head, Department of English, Osmania University, for his encouragement and for reading the translation.

* Rita Jacob Cherian, Head, Department of English, Women's Christian College, Madras, and her students, for their play-reading.

* E. Ravikumar for getting the manuscript typed.

* V. Ramnarayan, Akhila and Abhinav for their support and suggestions.

Characters

NATH DEVALIKAR
JYOTI
JAYAPRAKASH
SEVA
ARUN ATHAVALE
HAMEER RAO KAMLE
VAMANSETH NEVRGAONKAR

Act One

Scene One

Between ten and eleven in the morning. An old block of a building in a middle-class colony. A drawing-room, small but neatly arranged. Pictures of Mahatma Gandhi, Acharya Narendra Dev, Yusuf Meherali and Sane Guruji hang on the walls. A few objets d'art representing different parts of India are placed in a manner which draws immediate attention to them. The general ambience of the drawing-room inspires calmness and confidence.

Nath Devlalikar, approaching sixty, yet appearing active, is on the telephone. Jyoti, going on twenty, and twenty-three year old Jayaprakash are his children; Jyoti is doing some secretarial work for her father, while Jayaprakash has dismantled a household appliance and is engaged in repairing it.

NATH: [*Almost shouting into the phone.*] Hello . . . At what time does the bus leave for Asangaon? . . . Hello . . . the Asangaon bus . . . Pune—Asangaon . . . Yes, yes, Pune—Asangaon . . . No bus service on that route? . . . How can that be? . . . Oh yes . . . Of course there is such a bus service . . . Tsk, I'm telling you . . . I have taken it! Yes, your own bus . . . This is Nath Devlalikar speaking . . . Member, State Legislative Council . . . Keep your greetings for later, first please take the trouble to inform me of the time of departure . . . What time? [*He puts the receiver down, frustrated.*] The line's got cut. First I couldn't get the number. When I got it, I couldn't hear anything. These people don't know a thing about their own bus service . . . And now the line's got cut! A strange business altogether! Tells me, the bus doesn't go there! Heaven knows who made him controller!

JYOTI: Why do you bother to ask each time? You know from experience that nobody answers properly. Besides, you leave only when it is convenient for you . . . And in general, your bus does take you there . . .

NATH: That's not the point . . . the point is that these people don't even have proper information about their own bus service.

JYOTI: And since when has it been possible to get information by making phone calls?

NATH: That's not the question. The controller must be fully informed about every single bus which departs from his terminal. After all, hasn't he been appointed for just this purpose?

JYOTI: Bhai, the way you talk, it's as if you have been specially appointed for the task of reminding all the people in the world of their duties.

NATH: Our Jayaprakash here, he has given us a new name—the repairers of the world! But you two are still young, you won't be able to understand. The visions we had of the future of this nation before Independence! And what we are forced to see today! Disgusting. It hurts. [*To Jyoti.*] Have you cleaned my lime juice flask? Last time my shaving brush was left behind . . . and . . . oh yes, the towel! How can I do without it? It's not nice to be somebody's guest and keep asking for trifles!

[*Jayaprakash mutters as he goes on with his work.*]

NATH: Well? What are you saying?

[*Jayaprakash remains silent. He looks at Nath and returns to his repair job.*]

NATH: Some damn thing or the other is always missing. In this connection the example of Vinobaji is worth following.

JAYAPRAKASH: [*As he works.*] It is rather late in the day to do that now.

[*Nath turns a questioning face to him.*]

JAYAPRAKASH: I mean, he is a confirmed celibate, isn't he? That's why he said . . . [*Gets involved in his work.*]

NATH: Celibacy has nothing to do with it, Jay! It is a matter of educating the mind. We must have discipline. But discipline has stayed miles away from us. Acharya Javdekar used to say, no doubt our Nath is intelligent, but he is a country bumpkin.

[*Jayaprakash begins to laugh half-heartedly, then stops midway.*]

NATH: [*Looking at him.*] Oh, come on, laugh! Don't hold back!

JAYAPRAKASH: I wasn't laughing. I was pulling the nail out.

NATH: Tell me, when is Seva arriving from Ahmednagar?

JYOTI: Ma was saying that if the rally ended by noon yesterday, she'd be here by night, or by eleven o'clock today.

NATH: I have to leave at twelve-thirty.

JYOTI: In that case you two are sure to meet.

NATH: Two weeks have gone by, and this hide-and-seek continues. When she goes to Bombay for a women's camp, I stay here to lecture in Pune. If she comes to Pune, I go to Aurangabad to take part in a rally for people's rights.

JAYAPRAKASH: Don't worry, Dad! The two of us are always here. We keep conveying your messages to each other.

NATH: That's just it! Sending messages to one another cannot be called marriage. Isn't there a thing called co-existence? Eh? This is all too much of a rush, baba! This matter will have to be reviewed seriously sometime.

JYOTI: First the rush and scramble must stop. For both of you.

NATH: Right! Packed that medicine bottle of mine, have

you? Otherwise . . .

JYOTI: I've packed it.

NATH: Thank you, thank you. If the stomach is not in order, speeches becomes worthless. Nothing strikes the mind.

[*Jayaprakash gets up and goes inside.*]

JYOTI: [*Hesitantly.*] Bhai, I want to tell you something . . .

NATH: Tell me something? Say it then. Who stops you? We have a democracy in this house and we are proud of it. Democracy outside and dictatorship in the home, we don't know these two-timing tricks. I am all ears. Go ahead!

[*He sits down ready to listen.*]

JYOTI: [*With greater hesitation.*] Ma, . . . well, she should be here any time now. I have . . . something . . . to tell you both. Something about myself.

NATH: Very good! Tell me!

JYOTI: No. I want both of you to be there . . . only then . . .

NATH: [*Laughing.*] All right! All right! Seva will be here pretty soon . . . [*Looking at the clock.*] How much time will you take? Half an hour?

JYOTI: Fifteen minutes.

NATH: That's all? Granted! You are responsible for your mother being here . . . If she gets delayed, then . . .

JYOTI: For the last fifteen days I've been telling myself over and over again that I should speak to both of you, together.

NATH: Looks as if you have done a lot of preparation!

JYOTI: If you two can be brought together, only then . . .

NATH: That's true. We never seem to be able to sit down with you children, and talk . . . And that is bad.

JYOTI: Great! You do something, and then say it is bad. Why don't you leave the complaining to us!

[*Jayaprakash appears hurriedly putting his shirt on as he moves towards the front door.*]

JAYAPRAKASH: Ma has come . . . I'll bring the luggage in.
  [*He goes out leaving the door open.*]
NATH: Thank God she has arrived on time. [*Gets up eagerly.*]
  [*Jyoti walks to the front door. Seva enters.*]
JYOTI: [*Hugging Seva as she enters.*] Ma . . .
  [*Nath looks on.*]
SEVA: [*Patting Jyoti's back as she looks at Nath.*] I thought
  you would be gone!
NATH: I beg pardon for dashing your hopes. But the bus
  leaves at one-thirty.
SEVA: Ah! So the bus is late and that's why you are still
  here.
NATH: You're absolutely right! You think I'd wait for a
  mere wife! The call of the nation is far more important
  than the call of a wife.
  [*Jayaprakash enters with the luggage and goes inside.*]
SEVA: Not the call of the nation, Nath, it is the craze for
  speechmongering!
NATH: All right! Put it that way if you like. One certainly
  likes to hear one's own voice.
JYOTI: And that's not right. Go on, say it, say it yourself!
  You do all these bad things and then sit in judgement
  upon your self and say they are bad! And you proclaim
  you are democratic!
SEVA: He, a democrat! Ask me. If he had been democratic,
  would I be his wife?
NATH: Wait. You had total liberty to make your own
  decision!
SEVA: Yes. But if I had refused him, this fine gentleman
  would have shaved off his hair and journeyed to the
  Himalayas.
NATH: That would have been my problem. Who are you
  to . . .
SEVA: Nath, in the Englishman's language this is called
  'blackmail'.
NATH: Aha! Did you agree to get married because you

were frightened of my threats?

SEVA: You mean, it was my decision?

NATH: Let me tell you something, Jyoti. In those days two or three up-and-coming leaders were interested in her. And I! compared to them, there I was, nothing but a third or fourth rank worker. But yes sir, it was I who was chosen!

JYOTI: [*In Nath's tones.*] And it is just too bad!
[*Everybody laughs. Jayaprakash comes with a glass of water and stands before Seva.*]

SEVA: [*Sips.*] At that time I thought this man was 'all right'. Could become a minister or something. If he did, then there would be a chance for me to show off a bit. But no. It was all just bang-bang fizzzz! The Janata party comes into power and loses it, but this man stays an ordinary MLA!

NATH: Just you wait! Let our Socialists get hold of the government, and then—watch out! Who else is there to take the chair?

JAYAPRAKASH: [*Somewhat softly.*] Your dreams and mine!

NATH: Yes, yes! Dreams indeed! We do believe in miracles. [*Looks at the clock and remembers.*] My God! [*To Seva.*] Seva, our Jyoti here, she wants to tell us something. To us means—to you and to me. And we are simply never able to meet these poor children together. Therefore this girl has taken an appointment with us today. Fifteen minutes. [*To Jyoti.*] Only fifteen, right . . .? We will now talk to her. Sorry. We will listen to her . . . [*To Jyoti.*] Right? Yes. So now [*To Seva.*] Seva, please sit down calmly for fifteen minutes. I [*Sitting on the chair.*] sit here. [*Looking at Jayaprakash.*] And this gentleman? [*To Jyoti.*] Shall we let him stay here?

JAYAPRAKASH: I am making tea. [*Goes in.*]

NATH: [*To Jyoti.*] Shoot! [*To Seva.*] How was it? I mean, how was the women's rally? Were they good? Were the women receptive?

SEVA: Not all of them but three or four certainly were. They took part seriously. They seemed to be receptive.

NATH: Three or four! Not bad! Not bad at all. In our activists' camp, everyone was over fifty, I mean old codgers! As for the young men, well, there was Vaman Barve, aged forty! And the song? *Uthao jhanda bandaacha*—'Hold high the flag of revolution!' Damn it! How could he hold the flag of revolution? One must have the strength to hold it up! Poor fellow, he complains of a slipped disc!

[*Jyoti is standing and listening.*]

NATH: [*To Jyoti.*] Yes? What are you waiting for? Oh, oh, oh! I am sorry. No, no, extremely sorry. Really, Jyoti! We made a mistake . . . [*To Seva.*] We sat down to listen to her and we ourselves . . . [*To Jyoti.*] Jyoti *beta*, I apologize. Now you start.

SEVA: [*Getting up.*] Can I go for a little wash? I'll be back in a minute.

NATH: [*Holding Seva's hand to restrain her.*] No! No means no. Then it will be time for me to go and the poor girl will have to wait once again for the two of us to be together. Nothing doing. We listen to Jyo! [*To Jyoti.*] Begin!

JYOTI: No—no! If mother wants, let her have a wash.

NATH: *No!* First we listen to you, everything else afterwards. We do so much for the world, and we don't have time for our own children?! We should be ashamed to call ourselves your parents.

SEVA: All right, I have sat down . . . Why waste time in unnecessary blabber! Now, for a change, listen! Go on, Jyoti.

JYOTI: [*Hesitating again.*] I don't even know if it is a matter of such importance or not. I am still unable to make up my mind . . . that is . . . I have decided to get married.

NATH: [*Excited.*] Congratulations!

SEVA: [*Surprised.*] Decided!

NATH: Why? If she has made a decision, what is your
objection to it? She is a major now. Not a child any
more.

SEVA: When did I say she is a child? Only, it struck me
that . . .

NATH: What?

SEVA: I didn't call her a child. You know all this was not
expected. I only thought that . . .

NATH: What did you think? Your young daughter will stay
single all her life?

SEVA: [*Sounding fed up.*] You find a distorted meaning in
every ordinary statement.

NATH: That's why I've lasted so long in politics.

SEVA: Don't thrust your politics into the house. Listen to
her.

NATH: That's precisely what I'm doing. It is you who got
me into an argument. [*To Jyoti.*] Yes. Go on, Jyoti!
Who is the boy? Who is the prince charming?
[*Jayaprakash comes in with the tea-tray.*]

SEVA: [*To Jayaprakash.*] Jayaprakash, grace us with your
presence. Good news. Our Jyo is getting married. Jyoti,
tell us—who is he? Don't make us wait.
[*Seva becomes serious.*]

JYOTI: [*Both diffident and serious.*] His name is Arun
Athavale.

NATH: [*Wind out of his sails.*] A brahmin?

JYOTI: No, he is a dalit.

NATH: [*Excited.*] Marvellous! But the name sounded like a
brahmin's.

JAYAPRAKASH: Why? What if he were a brahmin?

NATH: I know. I know it doesn't make a difference. But if
my daughter had decided to marry into high caste, it
wouldn't have pleased me as much . . . Well, I'm telling
you the absolute truth.

JAYAPRAKASH: This is also a kind of casteism, isn't it?

SEVA: [*Soberly.*] Be quiet, Prakash! [*To Jyoti.*] What does he
do? Where does he live?

JYOTI: Right here, in Pune. He is doing his BA. He works
part time in 'Sramik Samachar'.

SEVA: Where did he meet you?

JYOTI: In the Socialists' study group. He has been coming
there for the past two months.

SEVA: His parents, what do they do?

NATH: I object to this question. His parents' occupation
has no bearing on the boy. The boy should be our
only concern.

SEVA: My question concerns the boy.

JYOTI: His parents live in a village. There is a village called
Chiroli near Karhad. They have a bit of land there . . .

SEVA: How many children do they have?

JYOTI: Seven. Arun is the second.

SEVA: [*Breaking a pregnant silence.*] What does his elder
brother do?

JYOTI: Nothing.

SEVA: Why?

JYOTI: He's like that, Arun says. His father works in the
fields, but it is not enough. Arun has to send money
home every month.

SEVA: The other brothers, what do they do?

JYOTI: When it's possible they go to school. The truth is
that they too don't do anything.

SEVA: There must be debts as well?

JYOTI: Must be. I think so. How much, I haven't asked.

SEVA: Then the entire responsibility of the family falls on
Arun's shoulders.

JYOTI: Yes.

NATH: A typical picture of those people. What is so special
about that?

SEVA: Will you or will you not let me speak?

NATH: What do you mean? I am allowing you to speak . . .
But if he is a boy from the dalit community . . .

SEVA: Do you think I am not aware of these things? [*With Nath silent, she turns to Jyoti.*] How long have you known him?

JYOTI: About two months.

SEVA: Is the boy intelligent?

JYOTI: He is, but not exceptionally so. He writes poems. I like them.

NATH: See, it's as if the boys of this community are endowed from birth with the genius for writing poetry.

JYOTI: Now he is writing his autobiography. I have read some parts of it. I felt that I could do anything to make him happy.

NATH: Great, Jyoti!

SEVA: [*To Nath*] Will you please allow us to talk? [*To Jyoti.*] What is he like as a person?

JYOTI: I won't say that he is the embodiment of all good qualities, but in my experience until now, there has been nothing bad.

SEVA: Is he trustworthy?

NATH: Objection! If he had not been trustworthy how could my daughter have chosen him? Do you mean that being a dalit, he . . .

SEVA: His being a dalit is not the issue here. I must know only whether he can be trusted or not.

JYOTI: I feel that he can be. His poems and his autobiography have inspired me with complete faith in him.

SEVA: And simply on the strength of this stock you have made up your mind to marry him!

NATH: Did you have any guarantee before we were married that I was trustworthy? We took part in the Socialist movement. What more did we have to go by?

SEVA: That was a different matter. I had been keenly observing you, from a distance of course. Don't mix these two things. [*To Jyoti.*] Jyoti, in my opinion you are acting in haste. Not even two whole months have passed since you two got acquainted. You don't have a clear and complete understanding of the man. And whatever you have is not anything to get excited about.

NATH: Therefore wait for two, or even three or four years. Gather the minutest bits of knowledge about the man. Study the depths of that knowledge. After that, think about marrying him. Nonsense!

JAYAPRAKASH: What is nonsensical about it, Bhai? Marriage, after all, is a knot tied for a lifetime.

NATH: Jayaprakash, do you know what it is to love at first sight? Tsk . . . studying is of no help here, this is a matter of plucking the heartstrings. If it rings here, it echoes there!

JAYAPRAKASH: But Jyoti is not saying that her heartstrings have been playing music!

NATH: That's exactly what must have happened, Eh, Jyoti? [*Jyoti shakes her head to say no.*]

JAYAPRAKASH: [*To Nath.*] See!

NATH: [*To Jyoti.*] You mean you didn't fall in love?

JYOTI: I don't know. Arun asked me, isn't the very idea of marrying me dreadful to you? I said, what is dreadful about that? Arun said, you don't think that I am an absolutely worthless fellow? I said, no! He said, this is incredible, and added, in that case let us get married. And I nodded.

NATH: [*As if his hopes have been dashed.*] No surge of intense feelings in your heart? [*Upon Jyoti's shaking her head.*] No rainbow-hued notes played upon your nerves? [*Upon her shaking her head again.*] No storm of hidden passions . . .? [*She shakes her head again.*]

JYOTI: I too am surprised. It was as if someone had asked, 'Shall we have some tea?' After that I kept feeling that it was all my imagination.

SEVA: [*Becoming serious.*] Jyoti, decisions about one's life must not be made so lightly.

JYOTI: I think I was fairly serious at that time.

SEVA: Do you think you have done a wise thing?

JYOTI: Sometimes I do. Sometimes I think I have acted like
         a fool.

SEVA: You have been very hasty, Jyoti . . .

NATH: This conclusion you have come to, is this not
         hasty? Right now we haven't even seen if the boy is
         dark or fair . . .

         [*Seva shows her displeasure.*]

NATH: Tell me if I'm wrong. Say it out.

JYOTI: I intend to invite him home when both of you are here.

SEVA: Of course we will see him when he comes. But
         when a girl thinks of marriage, she has to look for
         some kind of stability. For some compatibility in
         lifestyles. After all, it is a matter of a lifelong
         relationship.

NATH: If they decide to do so, lifestyles can certainly be
         changed. And the ideal of stability can be different for
         every man. After all, he is doing his BA, why won't he
         be able to stand on his own feet?

SEVA: What kind of a question is this 'why'? Look at his
         financial responsibilities also . . .

NATH: In case he is not able to fulfil his responsibilities,
         our Jyoti will start earning. She is no homebound
         housewife.

SEVA: [*Slightly irritated.*] Why are you arguing in the boy's
         favour even before looking at him? Why are you in
         such a hurry over Jyoti's wedding?

JAYAPRAKASH: Bhai, that is true enough . . .

NATH: All right. It is time for my bus. I'm going . . . Well,
         have we passed the resolution? We shall wait until we
         get to meet the boy. But what do we do after that? [*To
         Jyoti.*] You have made your decision. You have, haven't
         you?

SEVA: It is possible to reconsider it.

JYOTI: I don't know. But I do want to know your opinion.
         Actually, I should have done this much earlier, but

things happened suddenly, they did . . .

NATH: Doesn't matter, Jyo, don't worry. We are all with you. Prakash, go on, pick up my bag, let's look for a rickshaw.

[*The two of them go inside.*]

SEVA: [*To Jyoti.*] My anxiety is not over his being a dalit. You know very well that Nath and I have been fighting untouchability tooth and nail, God knows since when. So that's not the issue. But your life has been patterned in a certain manner. You have been brought up in a specific culture. To erase or to change all this overnight is just not possible. He is different in every way. You may not be able to handle it.

JYOTI: I will manage, mother!

SEVA: Saying something is easy, but doing it is very difficult . . . And later there is no chance for a woman to hide or to run away.

JYOTI: It doesn't seem to me that I would run away.

SEVA: Think very carefully and decide. That's my advice.

JYOTI: I understand all that you are saying, mother. But whatever has happened, and how it did happen, is something that even I don't quite understand. Today when I wonder and think about it, I realize the seriousness of it.

SEVA: This is not very wise.

JYOTI: Certainly not. And yet what has happened has happened.

SEVA: But the decision can be changed.

[*Jyoti wants to say something. By then Nath and Jayaprakash come out with the bag.*]

NATH: All right! Ta-ta! I'm going. [*To Seva.*] How much longer will you light up this place? .

SEVA: I am here the whole week. On the thirteenth there is the Vidyavardhini Trust meeting in Bombay.

NATH: That's wonderful! This means I shall get ample time to settle all my work in Ahmednagar. I shall be back by the thirteenth evening. I remember I have to attend a meeting as soon as I arrive. Bye then, carry on, Jyo . . .

[*He pats Jyoti and goes out. Jayaprakash follows with the bag.*]

SEVA: [*Thoughtful.*] Jyoti, may I ask you a question?

[*Jyoti signals 'yes'.*]

SEVA: How close is this relationship? To put it bluntly, how far has it gone?

JYOTI: No, nothing like that! We meet, we talk, that's all.

[*Seva lets out a sigh of relief. But she is restless.*]

SEVA: All right! Let me put my things away. I've been sitting here since I came.

JYOTI: Ma, I've given you a lot of trouble, haven't I?

SEVA: Silly girl! . . . Whom can you trouble if not your mother . . .? But really, I am worried about you.

JYOTI: Sorry, Ma! Already you and Bhai have so many problems to face. I have added one more to them . . .

SEVA: [*Patting her.*] You're crazy! How can you children ever become a burden to us?

[*Jyoti goes in. Seva stands lost in thought for a few minutes. The telephone rings. At first it does not register. Then she goes and picks up the receiver. She talks into the phone.*]

SEVA: Hello? Who is it, Kusum? Tell me, what's it this time? The women have no work on hand? Have we completed the Godrej order? All right, call the manager of Mehta Company and try. Tell him that the women are out of work, any kind of work will do . . . Yes, he knows about the kind of work we do. He will think of something. He will get annoyed, but he will do it for us . . . [*Listens.*] We have to think about this matter of Sunderbai . . . her behaviour is not satisfactory.

[*As Seva continues to talk on the phone, the stage slowly darkens.*]

* * *

Act One

Scene Two

Evening.
*Same drawing room. There is no one there. The front door is
opened with a latchkey. Jyoti comes in. Behind her Arun
Athavale enters. Aged 24–25. Complexion dark.*
*It is a harsh face, yet it is good looking. When they come in,
Jyoti shuts the door. Both Arun and Jyoti are aware of the door
being shut and of their being alone in the house. Their eyes
meet unintentionally. Both hesitant.*

JYOTI: [*Trying to sound natural.*] Sit down. Do sit down.
Everyone seems to be out on some work or the other.
Should be back any time.
[*Arun goes towards the sofa; sits down. A weight on his
mind.*]

JYOTI: Jayaprakash . . . my elder brother . . . is doing MSc.
He returns around five o'clock. Ma will come at about
five-thirty. She said so. But Bhai was going to be at
home, perhaps he had to go out somewhere. [*She looks
here and there and finds a note.*] Oh, he's left a note. 'I
should return by five-thirty, but I'm not sure.' In fact,
it will be a blessing if he returns by six-thirty. But
today he will definitely be here. You know he is very
eager to meet you. Wait, I'll be back in a minute. Just
a quick wash. [*Starts to go.*]

ARUN: Jyoti!

JYOTI: [*Stops.*] Yes?

ARUN: Sit with me, please.

JYOTI: Why? [*Moving towards him.*] I'll come in a

minute . . .

ARUN: I feel uncomfortable in big houses . . .

JYOTI: Feel uncomfortable? Why? This is not a big house.

ARUN: If you see my father's hut you'll understand. Ten of us, big and small, lived in that eight feet by ten feet. The heat of our bodies to warm us in winter. No clothes on our back, no food in our stomach, but we felt very safe. Here, these damn houses of the city people, they're like the bellies of sharks and crocodiles, each one alone in them!

JYOTI: Our house is not like that.

ARUN: Last night I was with Nikhil in the hostel. He was explaining dialectical materialism. It was late so he said, stretch yourself out here. He fell asleep at once but I stayed awake. What if the building swallowed me up in the blink of an eye? What's the guarantee that it won't happen?

JYOTI: Nonsense! How can it happen? It is quite some time since you left the village and came to the city. Besides, now it is not even night, but bright, broad daylight!

ARUN: What difference does that make? These large buildings are just like crocodiles and sharks, whenever they want, they can gulp you down.

JYOTI: I can't understand this. Some people are scared of thieves, some of bandits, some of ghosts. But how can anyone be scared of a house? On the contrary, one feels safe indoors.

ARUN: As for me, I feel safe on the street. The bigger the crowds, the safer I feel. My heart shudders when walls of cement and concrete surround me. I feel I must get up, run, get lost in the crowd.

JYOTI: All right, I'll put the kettle on and come right away.

ARUN: Don't put it on.

JYOTI: What do I do then?

ARUN: Sit here, with me.

JYOTI: All right, let's do this. I'll make tea, you sit in the kitchen and talk to me.

ARUN: No, men who sit and chat in the kitchen are pansies! We will sit right here ... You sit here.

JYOTI: [*Somewhat shocked.*] All right.

ARUN: You are surprised. You must be thinking, 'What kind of a man is he!'

JYOTI: No, no. Not at all.

ARUN: You must also be thinking, 'What a bore the bugger is!'

JYOTI: Why do you say that?

ARUN: You'll think that. Because that's my manner. A scavenger's manner.

JYOTI: Don't say that!

ARUN: Our grandfathers and great grandfathers used to roam, barefoot, miles and miles, in the heat, in the rain, day and night ... till the rags on their butt fell apart ... used to wander shouting 'Johaar, Maayi—baap! Sir-Madam, sweeper!' and their calls polluted the brahmins' ears.

JYOTI: Arun ...

ARUN: Generation after generation, their stomachs used to the stale, stinking bread they have begged! Our tongues always tasting the flesh of dead animals, and with relish! Surely we can't fit into your unwrinkled Tinopal world. How can there be any give and take between our ways and your fragrant, ghee spread, wheat bread culture?

JYOTI: Arun ...

ARUN: Will you marry me and eat stinking bread with spoilt dal in my father's hut? Without vomiting? Tell me, Jyoti, can you shit everyday in our slum's village toilet like my mother? Can you beg, quaking at every door, for a little grass for our buffaloes? Come on, tell me!

[*Jyoti covers her face with her hands.*]

ARUN: And you thought of marrying me. Our life is not the Socialists' service camp. It is hell, and I mean hell. A hell named life.

[*Jyoti is weeping.*]

ARUN: Sorry! Mood's out! Happens often, but new to you. At times a fire blazes—I want to set fire to the whole world, strangle throats, rape and kill. Drink up the blood of the beasts, your high caste society. Then I calm down like the taantric when he comes out of his trance. Like a corpse, I live on. I've made you suffer, I'm sorry. What am I but a troublemaker . . .

[*Jyoti's weeping has stopped, but her face is still hidden.*]

ARUN: Didn't I say I'm sorry? Anyone walking in now will say who knows what the bugger did. They will push me out of the door. No loss to me. It's your marriage which will fizzle out. That okay by you?

[*Jyoti removes her hand from her face and wipes her tears.*]

ARUN: *Hasli re hasli, ek baamaneen fasli!*—'It's a jolly game, Caught a brahmin dame'.

[*Jyoti laughs. Opening the door with a latchkey Jayaprakash enters. Sees them and is embarrassed. He shuts the door.*]

JYOTI: [*Hearing the sound of the door closing.*] Oh! Jayaprakash?

[*Jayaprakash still feeling embarrassed, is about to go inside.*]

JYOTI: Wait! this is Arun. [*To Arun.*] My brother Jayaprakash.

[*Arun and Jayaprakash greet each other formally. Looking at Jyoti, Jayaprakash realizes she has been crying.*]

JAYAPRAKASH: [*As he goes in.*] Just a minute. [*Goes in.*]

JYOTI: [*Smiling as she wipes her eyes.*] God knows what he must have thought.

ARUN: Just this, that I beat you.

JYOTI: [*In a soft, caressing voice.*] Just look at the wife-beater!

ARUN: Why? Why? Is it so difficult to beat you?

JYOTI: I am not one of those delicate touch-me-not creatures. I belong to the Seva dal tradition.

[*Before Jyoti can guess what's coming, Arun grabs her arm and twists it. Jyoti moans in pain.Shock greater than pain. Arun does this in a split second. Jyoti doesn't know now to react. She is confused and hurt. Lump in her throat. She tries to blow upon the arm to reduce the pain.*]

ARUN: Sorry . . . Don't know what came over me. So sorry. Give me any punishment you like . . . I'll take it . . . When anyone throws a challenge at me, I lose all control . . . Did it hurt so much? Let me see . . .

[*Seva who has opened the door with a latchkey enters and watches this little drama. Both look at Seva. Jyoti comes to herself.*]

JYOTI: Ma, you've come! This is Arun . . . Arun, my mother.

[*Arun folds his hands to greet Seva. It doesn't seem as if Seva is pleased to see Arun. Arun goes into a shell.*]

JYOTI: Ma, Prakash has come . . . he's inside.

[*Jyoti and Arun are standing.*]

SEVA: [*Coming forward and looking at them both.*] Why are you standing? Please sit down. Jyoti, when did Nath go out? He said he would not go. When will he return?

JYOTI: [*Not totally in control yet.*] He was not here when we came. Left a note, saying he'd come by five-thirty. Here . . . [*Searches for the note. It cannot be immediately located*].

SEVA: [*Watching Jyoti's frantic movements.*] Never mind. Did you make tea for Arun?

JYOTI: No. Didn't get the time. [*Their eyes meet.*]

SEVA: If someone comes to your house for the first time, shouldn't you offer him some tea? Go, put the kettle

on. One cup for me too . . . and bring something to
eat. Nath had brought some biscuits yesterday. They
are on the shelf, in the top jar. And listen, send
Prakash here.

> [*Jyoti goes in muttering 'yes'. Arun sits in his place,
> restless and nervous.*]

SEVA: [*To Arun.*] Jyoti was saying you're doing your BA.
> [*Arun stays silent.*]

SEVA: What are your subjects?
> [*Arun answers but continues to be restless.*]

SEVA: What are you going to do after that?

ARUN: After what?

SEVA: After passing your BA, what will you do?

ARUN: Haven't decided on anything.

SEVA: You will have to make a decision. What is the use
of a mere BA?

ARUN: No use at all.

SEVA: Nowadays no one looks at a BA.
> [*Arun tight-lipped, restless.*]

SEVA: There is some scope in science and commerce. But
really, nowadays even that isn't anything special. So
much competition . . .
> [*Arun is getting bored.*]

SEVA: There's no limit to rising costs. If you want an
ownership flat in Pune, you have to count out fifty or
sixty thousand rupees. Where do you live? You must
have your own place?
> [*Arun is fed up now. Shakes his head to say 'no'.*]

SEVA: It is no longer an easy thing to run a household.
Leaving aside the question of children for the present,
still, one must have at least a room to one's
name . . . Then there are illnesses, and so many other
problems. If one decides to get married, then, even if
not very much, still one needs a little money on
hand . . . If there's no money, there should be a stable
career at least. Otherwise one suffers, and the wife has

to suffer for no reason . . .

ARUN: [*Patience running out.*] We don't worry about such problems.

SEVA: You have to worry. How can anyone escape them?

ARUN: No problem. We shall be brewing illicit liquor.

SEVA: [*Shocked.*] What?

ARUN: Yeah. There's good money in brewing liquor—only you must know the technique.

[*Seva is shocked and silenced.*]

ARUN: It is a first class profession for two persons. The man bribes the police and the wife serves customers. People call her aunty. The more striking the aunty's looks, the brisker the trade . . .

[*Jayaprakash comes with the tea-tray.*]

SEVA: [*Coming out of her shock with effort, and changing the subject.*] Prakash, this is Arun Athavale.

JAYAPRAKASH: [*Coolly.*] I know. We were introduced just now.

ARUN: [*To Jayaprakash.*] I was telling her about this matter of brewing illicit liquor. [*With determined obstinacy.*] So I was saying that this business is highly profitable. Secondly, it is fun for the man and wife. Can take it easy. If there are children, there's work for them also, to wash glasses and plates, to fetch *paan* and cigarettes. And very good income in the tips. Many hands to work, and so many chances to rake in money. [*Arun is happy now seeing Seva's unrest*].

[*Jayaprakash tense. Jyoti enters. It doesn't take her long to guess at the state of things.*]

JYOTI: [*Forcing herself to smile.*] You know, Ma, sometimes Arun can take his jokes too far.

ARUN: [*To Seva and to Jayaprakash.*] Don't take her seriously. She met me only yesterday, or was it the day before? What can she know of me?

JYOTI: [*Trying to save the situation.*] I know everything.

ARUN: [*Abruptly.*] You don't know a shit. Shut up.

[*Everyone hit very hard. Jyoti extremely nervous. The calling bell rings very loudly.*]

JYOTI: [*Feeling relieved.*] Must be Bhai! [*Virtually rushes to open the door. Brightening.*] Look, Bhai is here!

NATH: [*Looking at everyone as he enters.*] Sorry. I got held up. A gentleman buttonholed me just as I was getting out of the party office. His grievance was genuine, couldn't put him off. Even so, I got off fairly early. [*Everyone solemn.*]

JYOTI: Bhai, this is Arun. [*To Arun.*] Arun, my father.
       [*Arun does not respond.*]

NATH: [*Coming forward and taking his hand.*] Very, very glad to meet you, young man! I have heard a lot about you. [*Winks at Jyoti.*] What I heard I shan't tell you. [*Looking at Arun from head to foot.*] Good. A man should be like this. . . Strong! He may break but he will not bend . . . Very good. [*To Jayaprakash.*] Jayaprakash, learn something from him . . . Our Jayaprakash is a tiger when it comes to work, but a lamb in everything else. A man must have some guts, you know! [*To Jyoti.*] Did you give him anything to eat? Seva, see, Jyoti has turned out to be luckier than you. What a manly fellow she's bagged! He is also creative, writes poetry. [*To Arun.*] Why don't you recite one of your poems to us?
       [*Arun looks worked up. Everybody else tense.*]

JYOTI: [*With effort.*] Bhai, shall I make some tea for you?

NATH: What do you mean? There is no meaning to life without tea. And make it two cups. [*Indicates Arun.*]
       [*Jyoti goes in. Nath makes Arun sit by his side, takes his hand.*]

NATH: I am really, really happy, Arun. Let us celebrate over a cup of tea. Well, nowadays our Socialists don't mind even liquor. But in this matter, I continue to be somewhat old-fashioned. A little worm called Gandhi ate into my brain in youth, didn't he, therefore certain

things slipped out of my life forever. Liquor is one,
fancy clothes is another, and [*In mock whisper.*]
something else. Celibacy would have been my lot, but
a mishap occurred. [*Winks at him.*] That, which they
call a sweet mishap. Just like it has happened to you.

SEVA: [*Gravely.*] Won't you go in and change your clothes?

NATH: Later. Seva, until today, 'Break the caste system'
was a mere slogan for us. I've attended many intercaste
marriages and made speeches. But today I have broken
the caste barrier in the real sense. My home has
become Indian in the real sense of the term. I am
happy today, very happy. I have no need to change my
clothes today. Today I have changed. I have become
new . . . [*To Arun.*] My friend, do you smoke? I don't,
but we have cigarettes if you like. Just the day before
yesterday Anu-ji returned, don't know which
international congress he had gone to attend . . . he
brought some packets of cigarettes. He said, take and
distribute . . . [*To Seva.*] Where are they? Get them, get
them . . .

    [*Seva goes in unwillingly.*]

NATH: [*To Jayaprakash.*] Why are you standing? Sit down.
Actually it is you two who should be chatting together.
You belong to the same generation. I am here like the
old stag who cut off his antlers to join the fawns.

    [*Seva brings the cigarettes and puts the packet down in
front of Nath.*]

NATH: Just one packet? What'll we do with the rest? Or
has someone finished them off? [*Gives Jayaprakash a
naughty look.*]

JAYAPRAKASH: [*Serious.*] I don't know.

NATH: I don't either. In that case it has to be . . . Seva or
Jyoti!

SEVA: Chhee!

NATH: Come on, what's wrong with you smoking? The
other day I read that the famous dancer, what's her

name—Sonal Mansingh—smokes cigars. Just imagine,
Arun, a dancer, a divinely beautiful, slim-waisted Indian
damsel with a cigar thrust into her mouth like
Churchill, who asks as she chews upon it, 'Oi loike
cigars, so what?' You see, in our times we wouldn't
even dare to dream of smoking cigars. If my father had
seen a cigar in my mouth, he'd have given me a hard
slap on the ear first and then said, 'You like cigars?
Well, get out! Out of my house.' And today Sonal
Mansingh boasts openly, 'I like cigars.' [*Whispering as if
sharing a secret.*] Not only this, she says 'And a good—'
you know what! [*Winks, then laughs whole-heartedly.*]
Well sir, times have changed indeed [*To Arun.*] Shall I
tell you something? Often when I sit alone and think,
it seems to me all that was a dream . . . everything
looks upside down. Just think, did it strike anyone that
you dalit people would stand up and flex your muscles
and challenge the Establishment as you are doing now?
Jyo! listen, bring something to eat, quickly. We're
starving to death here. [*To Arun.*] Our hunger is
enormous, just like the hunger of our Congress
friends . . . with this difference, that we eat only food.
[*He extends his hand to be congratulated. Arun does not
respond.*]

> [*Jyoti brings tea on the tray and plates with snacks.
> Puts them down.*]

NATH: [*Eyeing them.*] Good! good! That's like a good girl!
[*To Arun.*] Come on, come on, tea and snacks, don't
just look at them. Start, don't feel shy . . . [*He gives
Arun a plate.*] Hurry, otherwise it will all be finished.
[*Eating.*] Today I am very happy. [*Patting Arun on the
knee.*] Thank you, Arun, thanks for giving us the
pleasure. [*To Jyoti.*] Really, we must thank you too, but
you are one of us. [*Perceiving everybody's seriousness.*]
Oh, am I holding forth as usual? All right. I will rest
my voice box.

[*No one says anything even after he stops talking. Tension in the air.*]

ARUN: [*Getting up.*] I am leaving.

NATH: [*Surprised.*] Going? So soon? We were waiting to listen to one of your poems.

ARUN: Some work to do. [*To Jyoti.*] I'm going, Jyoti. [*Walks determinedly towards the door.*]
[*Jyoti follows.*]

ARUN: [*Opening the door.*] See you! [*Goes out, and without a backward look, pulls the door shut.*]
[*Explosive silence for a few seconds.*]

NATH: [*With displeasure.*] You people become hangdogs when it is not necessary. I don't understand it at all. How would he have felt?

SEVA: He felt nothing.

NATH: That is not correct. That boy had come to our house for the first time. Jyoti had brought him.

JAYAPRAKASH: That's why we tolerated him.

NATH: [*With righteous rage.*] Why? How does the question of tolerance arise?

SEVA: You know nothing.

NATH: What is it that I don't know? He is a good boy, he's bright . . .

JAYAPRAKASH: You don't know anything.

NATH: [*Worked up.*] Don't know, don't know . . . Come on, what is it that only you people know? Let me *also* know what it is.

SEVA: He is not someone who can fit in among us.

NATH: Why? He is a dalit, is that why?

SEVA: [*Sharply.*] Don't imagine you are the only one with a liberal soul among us. We too know what it is to look beyond caste.

NATH: Then what is it that prevents his fitting in here, in this home?

SEVA: His culture . . .

NATH: [*Breaking out in fury.*] What do you mean by that?

Manners and culture, are they your ancestral property?
He is a good boy . . . he is well behaved . . . can anyone
be that without culture?

JAYAPRAKASH: Bhai, you don't know everything.

NATH: Again the same thing? What don't I know?

SEVA: Nath, he was all right in your presence, but before
you came, what I saw him do, it was not right at all.

NATH: What did you see? Definitely your eyes must have
been prejudiced.

JAYAPRAKASH: Bhai, don't blame Ma without reason. What
I saw . . . and heard . . . was also not all right. You will
say that my vision too is tainted. You may say so. But
to me he didn't in any way appear to be good man. I
can't tolerate him. [*To Jyoti.*] Sorry, Jyoti. [*To Nath.*] If
you people hadn't been here, then either he, or I,
would have left this place . . .

NATH: [*With determination.*] Give me the details. Be specific.

JAYAPRAKASH: He was telling mother about brewing illicit
liquor.

NATH: So what? Brewing liquor is a hard fact in our
society.

SEVA: Would you like to know what he said to me . . .?
He wants to run a liquor den with his wife. He said
their children would be washing glasses and plates,
fetching *paan* for customers.

NATH: [*Shaken, but steadying himself.*] It is obvious that he
was joking.

JAYAPRAKASH: You should have heard him say it. He was
rudeness itself.

NATH: Delusions! Artificial Western civilities have become
a habit with us . . . so that we can't bear simple,
straightforward talk.

JAYAPRAKASH: Never mind me and Ma. Will you listen to
what he said to Jyoti? She tried to say something to
support him and he said 'You . . . [*Shrinking a
bit.*] . . . don't know a shit. You shut up!' Such obscene

language in this house, to a daughter of this house!
And in mother's presence?

NATH: [*Faltering a little but with renewed force.*] Don't go
by his language . . .

SEVA: Jyoti, what were you doing when I came in?

JYOTI: [*Scared.*] What . . .?

JAYAPRAKASH: When I came in there were tears in her
eyes . . . and he was clapping his hands and singing '*Ek
baamaneen fasli!*'—Caught a brahmin dame! She was
certainly weeping. Weren't you, Jyoti?
      [*Jyoti signals 'yes'.*]

JYOTI: [*Convinced of it being necessary to make some answer.*]
But it was not what you people imagine.

SEVA: I saw with my own eyes that you were blowing
upon your right elbow. What was the reason?

JYOTI: [*Haltingly.*] He had twisted my arm.
      [*Seva looks at Nath triumphantly.*]

JYOTI: Even this is not what you thought it was.

SEVA: Oho! He was twisting you arm for fun, was he?

JYOTI: No. But he did feel bad about it. He said sorry.
And he meant it.

JAYAPRAKASH: [*Sarcastically.*] He said sorry! Who can say
that he has no manners? When it is convenient they
become well-mannered.

NATH: Look, he is not a middle-class man like us to be
understood so easily . . .

SEVA: Yes sir, who are we to know anything about
someone who doesn't belong to the middle class?

NATH: Not only is he not a middle class man, he is a dalit.
He has been brought up in the midst of poverty and
hatred. These people's psychological make-up is
altogether different . . . We must try to understand him
and that is extremely difficult.

SEVA: If you like, I'm ready to attend your study circle on
this subject. But I will never accept him as my Jyoti's
husband. Never.

NATH: Look, Seva, society cannot be transformed through
words alone. We have to act as catalysts in this
transformation. The old social reformers did not stop
with making speeches and writing articles on widow
remarriage. Many of them actually married widows.
Why did they do it . . .? That was also an experiment, a
difficult experiment. But they dared to risk it.

SEVA: Does it mean that my daughter's life is to be used
for an experiment? Is that what you are saying? You
may have your views. I cannot accept them. I am her
mother. If you ask me I will say that Jyoti can never
be happy with that man . . . . If you like take it from
me in writing.

NATH: After all, how long was he here? On the strength of
what you learnt in that short time, you want to pass
judgement on him? Seva, you are acting in haste . . .

SEVA: May be. But Jyoti's marriage to him is out of the
question.

[*A tense pause.*]

NATH: [*To Jayaprakash.*] And you? Do you also feel the
same way, Prakash?

[*Jayaprakash signals 'yes'.*]

NATH: Jyoti, as I see it, only you can take in this whole
situation and say something more about it. Whatever
we may have to say, we are outsiders after all, and
where the boy is concerned, we hardly know
him . . . You tell us, what is your impression of the
boy? How does he appear to you? Forget for a little
while that you are thinking of marrying him, and give
us your objective assessment. It will help us to form
our own.

JYOTI: [*Diffident, immersed in thought.*] Bhai, I told you at
the outset . . . I don't know much about him. The little
I know of him is through his poems. He asked me, I
said yes, quite spontaneously. To tell you the truth, I
have been learning something of him only since then.

Not only getting to know him, but also getting to
know about him. And sometimes he shows such a
different side, that it strikes me, I don't know him at
all. At times I feel I can trust him, but the very next
instant I am left miles behind him. I ask myself—this
thing that I want to do, is it the right thing . . .? I am
afraid—then my own mind assures me that he is not
bad at heart, by nature he is not vile. He is complex.
Human beings are complex. It is possible that his
complexity has been generated by his circumstances. I
must understand that complexity. It is no use running
away. Once I understand it, I can dispel that
complexity. And even if I'm not able to dispel it, it
would no longer have the power to scare me.

NATH: Does it occur to you Jyoti, that you have perhaps
made a mistake in saying 'Yes'?

JYOTI: [*Pausing a little.*] Once in a while. But right or
wrong, what does it matter any way? I made a
commitment and now I can't run away.

SEVA: Why not? . . . A promise given in a weak moment
can certainly be reconsidered. If you find it difficult, we
can tell him on your behalf that . . .

JYOTI: I would hate to do that. I will marry him.

JAYA PRAKASH: Even if Ma doesn't like it?

NATH: [*At once.*] Prakash! Don't pressurize her! Let her
decide on the strength of her own judgement.

JAYAPRAKASH: The decision has been made thoughtlessly,
she herself has admitted it . . .

NATH: That she herself has said it means that she is
capable of thinking it over. With that she can change
her earlier decision.

JYOTI: I don't want to change it, Bhai.

SEVA: Jyoti, I tell you, don't let a wrong move spoil your
life.

JYOTI: Ma, my decision is final.

NATH: Not simply a matter of stubbornness?

JYOTI: No.

SEVA: Are you aware of the consequences?

JYOTI: Yes.

NATH: All right, then. Jyoti has made a decision for herself. All discussion on this subject is closed. Hereafter all of us must forget our differences of opinion and go along with Jyoti. Whatever support she may need, we must give whole-heartedly. What do you think, Jayaprakash?

JAYAPRAKASH: [*With effort.*] I will try.

NATH: Not just try. You must support her. We have practised democracy in the real sense in our home. This tradition should continue. Differences of opinion should be expressed, but the decision should be left to the individual. And the rest of us must provide support.

SEVA: Even after knowing that such a decision will prove disastrous?

NATH: Yes, even then. Whatever needs to be said should be said. After that we shall accept the decision knowing that it has been made with due consideration.

SEVA: Not by me, it won't be. You run your democracy. To me Jyoti's decision seems to be absolutely senseless, and as her mother I cannot accept it . . . This is a home, not your party where you can impose your discipline.

NATH: What do you intend to do?

SEVA: I will oppose this marriage. In your words I shall break party discipline and revolt. Does Jyoti's resolve seem sensible to you? Tell me, as a father, hand on heart. Don't beat around the bush.

JAYAPRAKASH: Yes Bhai, tell us frankly, what is your opinion?

NATH: I am on Jyoti's side. It is perfectly natural that the boy should have rough edges; they are the product of the circumstances he has endured. In fact it would be surprising if these peculiarities didn't exist. But just because he has them, it doesn't mean he's a bad fellow. He may not be a gentleman, but neither is he a scoundrel. As a human being he has potential. He has intelligence, drive and creativity. He has come so far despite his circumstances: this is not an easy matter. It is the result of his effort and dedication. You cannot imagine at what cost these people have made the little progress that they have. He is like unrefined gold, he needs to be melted and moulded. This is the need of the hour. Who can perform this task if not girls like Jyoti? Of course it is difficult, but it needs to be done. Besides, she has given her word. Remember, it is we who are responsible for the age old sufferings of these people. We have betrayed them for generations. We should feel guilty about this. And now if Jyoti breaks her word, if she wriggles out of her responsibilities, it would be a kind of treachery. It would amount to running away from the challenge. As a father I would feel ashamed if my daughter were to run away . . . [*Walks towards Jyoti and touches her gently.*] I am with you, Jyoti. What you are doing could be both wise and foolish. But one thing is certain. It upholds the norms of civilized humanity, and therefore, I stand by you. Go ahead my child, let us see what happens.

[*Darkness.*]

* * *

Act Two

Scene One

Same place. Some months later.
  The bell rings. Seva comes from inside and opens the door.
  Jyoti has returned from work. Tired and crushed. She appears thinner and as if she has suddenly become older. An ordinary mangalsutra round her neck. Jyoti comes in. Looks at Seva and starts to go inside.

SEVA: Where were you last night? If I may ask?

JYOTI: In Dinanath's room. It was very late so we slept there.

SEVA: [*Swallowing her anger.*] Couldn't you make a call to say you weren't coming?

JYOTI: He didn't have a phone in his room.

SEVA: And no phone in any hotel nearby? All of us kept awake the whole night.

JYOTI: [*In a tired voice.*] I have already told you ...

SEVA: [*Controlling herself from snapping.*] '... I have already told you. Don't wait. If I can—I will come, if I can't—I won't come ...' Jyoti, this is a home, not a hotel.
  [*Jyoti is about to go in without answering.*]

SEVA: This won't do. You belong to this house. Don't you know your responsibilities? I have been watching your strange behaviour ever since you got married. If you couldn't call at night you could have surely called during the day.

JYOTI: I was caught up in office work the whole day, didn't get any time ...

SEVA: Look, if it is difficult to remain a member of the

household, the best thing is to go one's own separate
way. You understand?

[*Jyoti looks at Seva to assure her that she has
understood. She is about to go in.*]

SEVA: You can torment me, but do you know, if you
don't return, Nath is unable to sleep. He keeps awake
late into the night worrying about you. Show a little
consideration at least for him. He was not against your
marriage. Why, he danced at your wedding as he never
did at his own.

JYOTI: This won't happen again . . . [*She turns to go.*]

SEVA: These words don't mean a thing. You keep saying it
won't happen but happen it will!

JYOTI: Ma, if it is in my hands this won't happen again.

SEVA: You can't get away with this excuse now. You got
married according to your own will. You proved that
you could do it.

JYOTI: Let it be, won't you Ma . . . Please! . . .

SEVA: After your marriage the atmosphere of this house
has changed. And do you think you have remained the
same, Jyoti? You live here like a stranger taking shelter
in this house out of sheer necessity. You are no help to
us, nor are we able to depend on you. You are lost in
yourself. If you go out we don't know when you will
return, and when you do return it is like this! Like a
stranger . . .

JYOTI: Didn't I say sorry . . .

SEVA: I don't accept it, I'm telling you.

JYOTI: What should I do . . . Shall I go away?

SEVA: This impertinence—it is not yours. We know very
well who puts you up to it.

JYOTI: I am not impertinent . . . And if I have been, it is
my own impertinence.

SEVA: [*Suddenly overwhelmed.*] How you have changed
Jyoti! For myself I have nothing to say, but the
sufferings Nath endures . . . [*She is able to control herself*

only with great effort.]
[*Jyoti doesn't know what to do. Jayaprakash comes out
from the inner room.*]

SEVA: He cannot concentrate on anything. He broods, day
and night.

JYOTI: [*Gently.*] May I go in now?

SEVA: Go wherever you like. Who can stop you?
[*Jyoti goes inside. Seva stands still for a while.
Perplexed.*]

JAYAPRAKASH: Ma, for how long will you and Bhai worry
yourselves sick?

SEVA: It cannot be helped.

JAYAPRAKASH: If you know that this is how things are
going to be, why worry?

SEVA: Saying that is easy.

JAYAPRAKASH: I don't understand why Bhai continues to be
distressed. He had not only approved the match, he
had also actively promoted it.

SEVA: You will understand when you have a daughter and
she grows up.

JAYAPRAKASH: If Jyoti has no complaints why do you get
upset?

SEVA: I said you won't understand. [*Depressed again.*] What
a home this was! What an atmosphere it had . . . !

JAYAPRAKASH: How can the same atmosphere always
prevail? Everything changes. Those who are able to
adjust to the changing conditions, survive. This is the
law of life.

SEVA: Our guruji did not teach us that we should change
with the circumstances. Rather he would say you can
change your circumstances. We have lived with the
proud conviction that it is we who bring about the
changes in our circumstances.

JAYAPRAKASH: That is the cause of your sorrows.
Conditions have their own rules for change, they don't
wait for anyone to change them.

SEVA: You are right. I understand now, but I cannot put it into practice.

JAYAPRAKASH: Jyoti made a decision on the basis of what she wanted, of her own free will. Whatever the consequences, it is she who will bear them. Tomorrow if I make a decision, then its consequences will have to be borne by me alone. How are you involved? Why should you trouble yourselves? You have looked after us in our growing years, that is more than enough. Now the responsibility for the future is ours.

SEVA: Still the heart aches, Jay.

[*The bell rings. Jayaprakash opens the door. Nath has arrived. Appears washed out. Jayaprakash takes his small overnight suitcase.*]

NATH: [*Putting the files on the table.*] Well, well, well! What's happening? How is everybody.

JAYAPRAKASH: Fine!

NATH: The whole day was one mad rush. Very hectic day. Objections were being raised all the time in the house. There was a walk out too . . . In between, for about half an hour, a noisy protest and much table thumping went on. And there was this crowd of people with problems. I barely managed to get a taxi at four o'clock and leave Bombay . . .

SEVA: You hardly slept last night. You got up early in the morning and caught the Deccan Queen. Today you should have really stayed in Bombay. At least there you could have slept undisturbed.

NATH: That's all right. After all, tomorrow is a holiday. Generally one can take a first class nap during the dull speeches at the session. Today this was not possible. Jayaprakash, a cup of piping hot tea? [*To Seva, as he remembers, anxiously.*] Is Jyoti back?

SEVA: She's back. A few minutes before you.

[*Nath relaxes visibly. Jayaprakash goes inside.*]

NATH: How is she? Is she all right? Anything out of the way?

SEVA: When I asked her she said they had both gone to a friend's house at night. It got late so they stayed there. Every day it's the same story! When I said we get anxious, she began to say 'Didn't I tell you not to worry?' They spent the night there. I let it go, but she could have come home in the morning. She could have called at least. Is there no telephone in her office?

NATH: May be she couldn't find the time . . .

SEVA: And here we keep on worrying ourselves to death, is that of no account? The state in which you left for Bombay this morning is no secret to me. She had no time even to make a phone call?

NATH: Look, Jyoti is a good girl. She cannot be unaware of our problem. In spite of that if she slips up then surely there must be a reason, a valid reason.

SEVA: I know all the causes and reasons. He's the reason . . . . . . He!

NATH: May be. In that case we have to accept the situation. Jyoti has married him.

SEVA: You may accept it . . . You were yourself the wedding priest!

NATH: What should I have done? Tell me.

SEVA: We should not have allowed this marriage to take place.

NATH: Seva, Jyoti was legally of age. Of her own free will she had decided to get married. Do you think our objections would have stopped her? The question was a matter of her choice. Who are we to prevent it?

SEVA: If the girl deliberately wants to fall into a pit, will you let her?

NATH: Yes, I'll let her fall. Undoubtedly I will let her fall into the pit. Look, I will tell her whatever I think, not once, but many times. I will try to change her mind. But if she still insists on jumping into that pit, I will not stop her.

SEVA: You won't stop that stupid girl who is your own

daughter?

[*Jayaprakash brings the tea-tray.*]

NATH: I won't prevent even you. But if you get hurt, I
will suffer with you. The values I uphold in my public
life are the values I live by in my personal life. I will
never use compulsion on anyone who is capable of
thinking. Never, never. And, moreover, to me Jyoti's
decision did not appear to be in the least bit wrong.

SEVA: And that's what keeps you awake every night.

NATH: [*Sipping his tea.*] Let us suppose she had married
someone who is not a dalit, or any other fellow instead
of Arun. Can you guarantee peaceful nights for us?
Every new relationship brings a problem in its wake.
After all she is our own daughter and it is only right
that it is our sleep which gets disturbed. [*To
Jayaprakash.*] Hello Jay, what's the news in your
college?

JAYAPRAKASH: [*In an undertone.*] Jyoti is standing there!
[*Looks in the direction of the door.*]

NATH: What? Jyo? [*Gets up and goes towards the door. Looks
in.*] Hey miss, is this how you eavesdrop on a
conversation between man and wife? You'll get a
beating! [*He compels her to come along with him and sit
by his side.*] Sit here. You could have come straight out.
Why this furtiveness? Come on, have some tea. I
haven't sipped it yet. Here!

JYOTI: No, you have it.

NATH: Do have some. All day I drink tea at the council
hall. All right, half–half, here. [*He forces her to drink
half the tea, drinks the other half. He looks at Jyoti as he
drinks and his eye falls upon her arm.*] How did you get
that mark on your shoulder?

[*Jyoti immediately hides her arm.*]

JYOTI: What mark ... Have your tea ... Finish it, won't
you .... [*Her eyes are filled with tears, throat blocked.
Trying to suppress tumultuous feelings.*] Please ... Bhai ...

[*Silence filled with grief. Jyoti gets up suddenly and rushes in.*]

NATH: Wait, Jyoti. Don't go.

[*Jyoti stops and keeps standing. Doesn't turn back.*]

NATH: Come here. I cannot bear to see you go weeping out of the room. It has never happened before.

[*She stands motionless in the same spot with her back to Nath. Tries to control herself.*]

NATH: We shall stop discussing this matter if you don't like it. But don't leave the room.

[*Jyoti sits on a chair where she was standing but with her back to the others. Silence for a while.*]

NATH: [*Getting up and pacing; thoughtfully.*] Jyoti, I am going to say something entirely different now. Think about it. Talk to Arun and let us know your decision after that. There is no hurry. You can take your time.[*Looking at Seva and Jayaprakash.*] It is a good thing that as usual we are all here together. And don't think I was struck by this idea now, all of a sudden. For many days I had been wanting to say it. In fact last night I had decided to tell all of you. That's why I returned from Bombay today. Jyoti, from now on, I want both of you to stay here. [*To Seva who hastens to object.*] Wait, wait! Let me finish what I have to say, after that everyone will be given the opportunity to voice his or her opinion. I will also tell you why I thought of it. Our Jyoti got married and Arun had expected to get a single room at least temporarily. Sometimes our calculations go wrong. So we decided that until definite arrangements were made for other accommodation Jyoti would stay with her parents, while Arun looked for a place. It is not possible to find a house in Pune unless you shell out a huge deposit. Nor is there any certainty as to when such a place would be found. I don't think it is right that after marriage a couple should stay apart for an indefinite

length of time, and especially that Arun should hole up
with a different friend each day. This house is our
own, it is not very big but nor is it too small. And
Jyoti has been living here. Another person can easily be
accommodated here. We can accommodate him. What
do you say, Seva?

[*Seva is silent. She has not liked the proposal at all, but
she doesn't reply.*]

NATH: Jayaprakash?

JAYAPRAKASH: [*Indecisively.*] Ji . . .

NATH: Jyoti, what do you say to my suggestion? You
don't agree?

[*Jyoti sitting in the same place, shakes her head three or
four times. Still has her back to the rest.*]

JYOTI: [*With effort.*] No . . . I don't agree. I don't agree at
all.

NATH: As usual you will have to give reasons for it.

JYOTI: There are no reasons, but it is not acceptable to me.

NATH: This is not the way we settle things in this house.
You have to give your reasons, Jyoti. I gave mine.
[*Jyoti does not answer.*]

NATH: No-no! You must tell us the reason, whatever it
may be.

JYOTI: [*Agitated.*] He . . . he will not enter this house.
Because . . . [*With great effort.*] I have left him . . . I am
not going back to him again . . . never.
[*Everyone stunned.*]

JYOTI: It's . . . all . . . over . . .

NATH: [*At once.*] No-no, Jyo! Don't tell me . . .

JYOTI: I must tell you, Bhai, I must. I am fed up with him.
Fed up! Fed up! [*She breaks into uncontrollable sobs. With
great difficulty she restrains herself.*]

NATH: [*Going up to her.*] What is it? [*Sitting down beside
her, when she doesn't want to talk.*] Tell me.

JYOTI: Don't pet me, Bhai. I will start crying and I don't
want to cry. [*In a quivering voice.*] I must learn to live

without tears. I mustn't even complain. It was I who
made the decision, I have to find my own strength to
bear this, alone . . .

SEVA: What exactly did happen?

JYOTI: I am not going to tell you. Don't ask me. [*She is
still trying to control her sobs.*]

JAYAPRAKASH: Did he beat you again?

JYOTI: [*Wiping her tears.*] That's not the matter.

NATH: Then, what happened? What happened to make you
arrive at this irrevocable decision?

JYOTI: [*Getting up and going in.*] I'm going—[*The telephone
rings. She speaks with unbounded hatred.*] Must be his
call.

NATH: [*On the phone.*] Hello! Nath Devlalikar. Who?
Arun? . . . Jyoti? She's here. I am Nath speaking. Yes,
she's here. I'll call her. Please wait. [*To Jyoti.*] Arun.
[*Jyoti picks up the receiver with great reluctance.*]

JYOTI: [*On the phone—in a lifeless voice.*] Hello!
[*Listens with anger on her face; she attempts to
maintain her self-control, bites her lip; she speaks after
listening for a long time.*] Thank you. I say thank you
so much. [*Bangs the phone down.*]

NATH: What was he saying?

JYOTI: Rubbish! [*Trying to steady herself she goes swiftly in.*]

JAYAPRAKASH: Seems to be totally disillusioned.

SEVA: What else could you expect?

JAYAPRAKASH: From the beginning he was like this. A
complete boor.

SEVA: [*To Nath.*] And you were inviting him to move in
here!

JAYAPRAKASH: Bhai, how did such a thing strike you? That
man—in this house?

NATH: [*Absorbed in thought, restless.*] I thought, whatever
has to happen, let it happen here before our
eyes . . . perhaps it would have worked as a kind of
restraint . . . But this development is extremely worrying

[*He paces and down.*] Something has to be done about
it. Something . . .

SEVA: What will you do? Put him on your lap and give
advice?

NATH: [*He suddenly loses control.*] Stop it, I say! Stop it! It
is a question of life and death for the girl and you
crack jokes? Irresponsible fools! [*He is trembling. Seva
and Jayaprakash stunned by this unexpected explosion.*]

JAYAPRAKASH: Bhai, Ma was not cracking jokes.

SEVA: Never mind, Prakash.

NATH: [*Cooling down.*] I know! I lost control. I apologize.
Seva, forgive me.

SEVA: I know your anguish.

NATH: [*With passion.*] Seva, let not this wonderful
experiment fail! This dream which is struggling to turn
real, let it not crumble into dust before our eyes! We
will have to do something. We must save this marriage.
Not necessarily for our Jyoti's sake . . . This is not just
a question of our daughter's life, Seva, this has . . . a far
wider significance . . . this experiment is a very precious
experiment.

SEVA: [*Dryly.*] In this matter my stand has been very clear
from the beginning. This marriage is really no marriage
at all. But since you ask for my help, I am with you.
Tell me what is to be done. I will do it.

[*The calling bell rings incessantly. Jayaprakash opens the
door. Arun has come; he is drunk.*]

ARUN: [*Standing at the door.*] Jyoti . . . Jyoti's here, isn't
she? Where is Jyoti? I must see Jyoti.

[*Jayaprakash refuses to respond.*]

NATH: [*Going forward.*] Arun? . . . Why are you standing
outside? Welcome. Come in.

Arun: No . . . it is Jyoti I must . . . [*Calling out*]
Jyoti . . . Jyoti . . .

NATH: [*Bringing him inside and making him sit down.*]
Wait. I will call Jyoti.

ARUN: I don't have the time. Call Jyoti. It is she I want to see.

NATH: [*To Jayaprakash.*] Tell Jyoti Arun is here.
[*Obediently Jayaprakash goes in.*]

NATH: [*To Arun.*] What will you have? But join us for dinner . . . since you are here anyway . . .

ARUN: No. I am not fit to have dinner with people like you.

NATH: Why do you say that? Seva, will you get dinner ready?

ARUN: No. I will see Jyoti and fall at her feet. I will beg her pardon. Don't want anything else.

JAYAPRAKASH: [*To Nath in a voice that Arun can also hear.*] Jyoti won't come out. She says, whoever has come, tell him to go away.

ARUN: [*Getting up.*] Hear that? Jyoti doesn't want see me. My Jyoti doesn't want to see me. My Jyoti is telling me to go away. It is not her fault, not her fault at all. It is I who am at fault. I am the offender, a great offender in her eyes. Whatever I do, I will not be forgiven. Never can I be forgiven. I am a great scoundrel, rascal, motherfucker, . . . I . . . I beat her, with these very hands. I beat her badly, with these very hands I beat her up. I beat Jyoti. I make her suffer. I behave worse than an animal. She will never forgive me, I know it. Jyoti, you are not destined for me, this is the truth, Jyoti. After all scavengers like us are condemned to rot in shit. But Jyoti, I loved you from the heart. My love is not false, Jyoti, it is true. With these hands I hurt you . . . I must break them, throw these fucking hands away. [*He takes a knife out of his trousers pocket.*]

NATH: [*Anxiously.*] Arun, put the knife away first . . . Here, what are you doing, Arun?

ARUN: No. I shall not stop. I will cut off my hands. Then at least she will believe that my love was true . . .

[*Seva is tense. Arun's threat does not affect Jayaprakash.*]

NATH: Prakash, the knife...

[*Jayaprakash goes forward and snatches the knife. Arun does not stop him.*]

ARUN: Give my knife back—let me tear my hands out—at least let me do this much for my Jyoti. Let me die... [*Repeating Jyoti's name, he sobs loudly.*] I am a wretch Jyoti... I am not fit to clean your shoes...

NATH: [*Perceiving the artifice which even drunkenness cannot hide.*] Arun, there is no need to put up a public show. Calm down, control yourself.

ARUN: My sins cannot be washed away...

NATH: Can this wailing wash them away? Be quiet. We are civilized people here. Behave yourself.

ARUN: Help me get Jyoti back... Please...

NATH: We'll see. First calm down. [*Upon Arun's sitting down quietly.*] Prakash, tell Jyoti I want her here.

SEVA: Wait, Prakash. [*To Arun.*] WHY DO YOU BEAT JYOTI?

ARUN: [*Penitence in his voice.*] Kick my face as punishment. Not that it can be any compensation.

SEVA: [*Self composed.*] I am asking you, WHY DO YOU BEAT JYOTI?

ARUN: [*Trying to answer.*] One is hot-tempered. Gets a little drunk too. She says something, then I say something. The fight begins. I can't bear it. I lose control over my hands...

SEVA: When you first came to our place before your marriage the same thing had happened. Remember?

ARUN: May be.

JAYAPRAKASH: Not may be. It happened.

SEVA: At that time Jyoti was not even your wife.

JAYAPRAKASH: And you were not drunk then.

ARUN: When have I claimed that I am civilized and cultured like your people? From childhood I have seen my father come home drunk everyday, and beat my

mother half dead, seen her cry her heart out. Even
now I hear the echoes of her broken sobs. No one
was there to wipe her tears. My poor mother! She
didn't have a father like Bhai, nor a mother like
you . . .

SEVA: This is no answer to my question. WHY DO YOU BEAT
JYOTI?

ARUN: What am I but the son of scavengers. We don't
know the non-violent ways of brahmins like you. We
drink and beat our wives . . . we make love to
them . . . but the beating is what gets publicized . . .

SEVA: Drunk or sober, wife-beating is called barbarism.

ARUN: I am a barbarian, a barbarian by birth. When have I
claimed any white collar culture?

SEVA: Jyoti is not used to this kind of barbarism.

ARUN: I am what I am . . . and shall remain exactly that.
And your Jyoti knew what I was even before she
married me. In spite of that she married me, she did it
out of her own free will.

SEVA: She thought you would improve after marriage.

ARUN: If she thought so your Jyoti is a stupid fool.

NATH: [*Curbing Seva from speaking.*] Seva, please! [*To
Arun.*] Arun, it's no use repeating the same accusations
over and over again. It is absolutely true that Jyoti
married you out of her own free will. [*The telephone
rings. He goes towards it.*] Therefore it is Jyoti's duty to
put all her strength into making it work. [*Picking up
the receiver.*] Hello, who's speaking? Durgadas? Where
are you speaking from? Delhi or Bombay? [*Listens
attentively.*]

        [*Jyoti has come out to stand at the inner doorway. Like
        the others Nath too sees her.*

NATH: [*On the phone.*] Well . . . well . . . yes, yes . . . I
see . . . These are her usual hoodwinking tactics, if you
ask me. It's a big lie and it is being spread
systematically. Don't tell me she is going to impose

Emergency. Okay, if you hear anything more let me know, will you? [*Putting the receiver down with his eyes on Jyoti.*] Well, Jyo! What do you intend to do?

JYOTI: [*She goes straight to Arun ignoring everyone on the way.*] We are leaving.

JAYAPRAKASH: Are you really going away with this man?

JYOTI: [*Firmly and calmly.*] Yes.

SEVA: [*Sarcastically.*] Have you thought it out fully this time?

JYOTI: Yes.

NATH: Let her go, Seva. She must go.
[*Jayaprakash gives the knife back to Arun.*]

ARUN: Thanks.

JYOTI: [*To Arun, in bracing tones.*] We are going.
[*She goes up to the front door and opens it. She signals to Arun with her eyes. Both go away. Seva breaks down. She drops into a chair.*]

NATH: [*Looking in Jyoti's direction.*] Jyoti, I feel so proud of you. The training I gave you has not been in vain. [*Suddenly dejected.*] If only I believed in God, then Jyoti, this is the moment I'd go down on my knees and pray for you . . .

[*Darkness falls gradually.*]

* * *

Act Two

Scene Two

Same place, a few months later. Nath is immersed in a book. Seva enters opening the front door with a latchkey. Comes towards Nath and sits down in front of him.

NATH: [*Putting the book away after reading the last page.*] Fantastic! Amazing! How many years it is since I have read anything so beautiful! [*Lost in a reverie; Seva before him, tense and disturbed*]. You must read it, Seva! I have not come across anything like this in years! Such a powerful autobiography. Hats off to Arun Rao! It moves you to the core without ever becoming sentimental. And how precise! If you overlook one or two episodes, there is no verbosity anywhere. And the language! Oh, we have forgotten to speak our own language. But this is our true, living language, utterly free from the impact of English. Belongs one hundred percent to our own soil. Great! I am overjoyed.

SEVA: [*Gravely.*] May I say something?

NATH: [*Sobering.*] Sorry. Yes, yes.

SEVA: I have just returned from Dr Khare's nursing home after getting Jyoti admitted there.

NATH: [*Getting up at once.*] Why? Our Jyoti is all right, isn't she?

SEVA: You can say that . . . But the bleeding has started again. She is in her sixth month now. I got her admitted to the nursing home to avoid complications later. Jyoti refused to come. She only came because I insisted. Kumud says there's nothing to worry about, but she must be kept under observation until evening.

NATH: What was the reason? Did Kumud say anything?

SEVA: What could Kumud say? He had come home drunk
as usual. Jyoti didn't say anything much. She said it
was no big matter. There's an internal wound in her
stomach. The neighbours told me not to allow the girl
to stay there. They said, take her away, he beats her
and even kicks her.

NATH: [*With righteous rage.*] But why? How does she
offend him? Why treat her like this?

   [*Seva is silent.*]

NATH: Such behaviour towards a pregnant wife! What
happens if she dies? Such heinous behaviour by
someone who wrote this beautiful autobiography? How
can he? Here in these pages he describes the
humiliations he has undergone with extraordinary
sensitivity . . . and the same man kicks his pregnant wife
on her belly? How . . . ? How dare he do it to her?
How dare he?

SEVA: [*Dryly.*] Look, this talk is not going to lead us
anywhere. Instead let us try to get out of the situation
without splitting hairs. By now it is clear that this man
doesn't want to work, he wants to remain a burden on
Jyoti. It is also obvious that he will never feel grateful
for her support. If you ask me, I have my doubts as to
whether these dalits understand what gratitude means.

NATH: Seva!

SEVA: If you can express your opinion, I too must have the
right to say what I want. You can't stop me. You
think that I sound idiotic, but these are my views. Not
the views of someone who sits at home, but of
someone who has gone out and worked for the
downtrodden all her life. The truth is that your dalit
son-in-law, who can write such a wonderful
autobiography, and many lovely poems, wants to
remain an idler. He wants his wife to work. And with

her money he wants to drown himself in drink, and
have a hell of a time with his friends. On top of that,
for entertainment, he wants to kick his wife in the
belly. Why not? Doesn't his wife belong to the high
caste? In this way he is returning all the kicks aimed at
generations of his ancestors by men of high caste. It
appears that this is the monumental mission he has set
out to fulfill.

NATH: Seva, please!

SEVA: In this mission, if she dies, if his wife dies, he can
get another wife. But our daughter, if she dies . . . do
we have another?

NATH: For God's sake, Seva!

SEVA: Wait. Let me finish . . . Therefore I have decided to
bring Jyoti here, to this house. Alone. Not with him.
To stay here, at least until her delivery. But that
obstinate daughter of yours refuses to give in. Just now
I tried to persuade her in all possible ways at Kumud's
nursing home . . . [*Suddenly breaks into uncontrollable
sobs. Controls herself somehow and wipes her tears
hurriedly with the saree's end.*] Sorry. She simply doesn't
agree. She told me to go away. 'Ma,' said she, 'Go
away and don't come again.' I don't know what more I
can do after this . . . she said she was going to return to
her filthy room in the slum this evening.

[*Nath distressed. The phone rings.*]

NATH: [*Wearily into the phone.*] Yes. I am Nath Devlalikar
speaking. Yes. I've read it. It's beautiful. A very
beautiful piece of work. You want to organize a public
discussion? Very good. It will be a good thing. Me?
No. I am an involved party . . . No, don't drag me into
this. I will be there as a member of the audience but
don't press me to speak. No sir, don't announce my
name. I won't speak. There's no shortage of speakers.
Ask Nanasaheb. There's Babasaheb. Give a copy to
P.L. If he reads it, he will be able to speak. If you like

I myself will request them. Please leave me out, please ... No—no. I am not committing myself. Take note of this! [*Puts the receiver down.*]

SEVA: You found it difficult to say no.

NATH: [*Upset.*] 'You must speak', he insists!

SEVA: You too would have liked to speak.

NATH: [*Angrily.*] Damn it. The book is so good.

SEVA: Shall I tell you what I'll say if they ask me to speak? I will say that in this excellent book, whatever the author has said about injustice and exploitation is hypocrisy of the first order. Because this man himself exploits my daughter. Like a shameless parasite, he lives on my daughter's blood, and on top of that he gets drunk and bashes her up. Constantly he taunts her about her caste and about her parents, heaping foul abuse on them for being highborn.

NATH: What did you say? Abuse? On us?

SEVA: Jyoti didn't tell me this, her neighbour did. She tells him 'You can hit me or call me anything you like, you can bash me up, but don't drag my parents' name into it.' To torment Jyoti he says that you and I ...

NATH: What does he say?

SEVA: Don't ask me.

NATH: No. Tell me. What does he say? Tell me.

SEVA: He says I ... am ... a procuress who supplies girls from the Seva dal to the Socialist leaders ... says he.

NATH: No! No ... don't tell me ... !

SEVA: He says a lot more; you won't be able to take it.

NATH: [*Losing control.*] And about me? What does he say about me?

SEVA: Let it be.

NATH: I must know. What does he call me? Come on, what does he call me?

SEVA: Don't ask me ...

NATH: Why don't you tell me? What does he say?

SEVA: I tell you, don't force me to say it ...

NATH: [*Grabbing her.*] No . . . Say it, say it I say . . . let me
know it . . . I must know . . .

SEVA: No.

NATH: [*Shaking her hard.*] What does he call me? What
does he call me?

SEVA: [*With tremendous effort.*] That you . . . you are not
Jyoti's father. Like guruji . . . an eunuch . . . her real
father . . . [*She cannot go on.*]
  [*Jayaprakash is at the door. He has opened it with the
  latchkey. He has the evening newspaper in his hand.*]

JAYAPRAKASH: [*Closing the door behind him; unable to
understand what has happened.*] Sorry . . . I walked
in . . . as usual . . . walked in.

NATH: [*Distressed and annoyed.*] It's all right. Wasn't
anything. I was just asking her . . .
  [*Jayaprakash takes in the situation and is caught in a
  dilemma. Starts to go in.*]

NATH: No need to go in. You can stay here . . .

JAYAPRAKASH: I wanted to show you something. Of course,
only if you are in the mood for it . . . Nothing
important, just a notion I had . . .

NATH: [*Recovering.*] Sure. Tell me.

JAYAPRAKASH: [*Showing him the newspaper.*] Here's a news
item.

NATH: News item? What news item?

JAYAPRAKASH: Nothing special. It says here that in the
Middle East the Israeli forces have launched a strong
offensive against the Palestinian guerillas. To stop the
guerillas from getting water and food, as also all aid and
shelter, the Israeli forces have been razing the villages
of Palestinian civilians. Not just the menfolk, but
innocent women and children have been mowed down,
monstrous violence has been unleashed upon
them . . . so it says here.

NATH: That's war, Jayaprakash.

JAYAPRAKASH: True. But I remember that some years ago,

Hitler's Nazi troops had inhumanly decimated the Jews.
It was you who had given me books to read on the
subject. I couldn't bear to read about it, but you
insisted 'Read, this is history, and you should know it.'
And today the Jews have become the murderers of
Palestinian women and children.

NATH: [*Perturbed.*] What do you want to say?

JAYAPRAKASH: Just this, that those who were being
massacred are now indulging in massacres.

NATH: Perhaps they believe that this is necessary as defence
strategy.

JAYAPRAKASH: Perhaps. It's possible that gunning down
women and children is essential for one's defence. But
this means that the very victims of violence may go on
to perpetrate the same brutal violence upon others.
Perhaps they get a peculiar enjoyment out of it.
Perhaps those who are hunted derive great pleasure in
hunting others when they get an opportunity to do so.
The oppressed are overjoyed when they get a chance to
oppress others.

[*Nath very grave.*]

JAYAPRAKASH: This means that we don't feel, 'Let others
not endure oppression like we do, at least not because
of us, and never by our hands'. On the contrary, the
moment one gets the chance one becomes a greater
tyrant . . . one persecutes others with a vengeance,
because one exults in doing that.

[*Nath perturbed.*]

JAYAPRAKASH: In other words, yesterday's victim is today's
victimizer. If he has been shot at yesterday, he shoots
today . . . Therefore, there is no hope of a man's
gaining nobility through experience, he can only
become a greater devil.

NATH: [*In a burst of emotion.*] It's all wrong, Prakash!
Absolutely wrong. It is madness to arrive at a perverse
conclusion on the basis of a single example. The

ordinary citizens of Israel will certainly raise an outcry
against such atrocities. You will see! You are denying
all of human culture and civilization. That culture, that
entire civilization which man has evolved over the
years . . .

JAYAPRAKASH: Not at all . . . I was only trying to
understand the behaviour of that bastard Arun.

    [*Tense silence.*]

NATH: [*Outraged.*] Prakash, take that word back.

JAYAPRAKASH: [*Eyes downcast for a moment, then.*] I was
wrong. I apologize.

NATH: You have been brought up with certain values! And
you! It is wrong to show disrespect to anyone, under
any circumstances. We are cultured and civilized.

    [*Jayaprakash quiet.*]

SEVA: Prakash did not say it deliberately. He said what he
felt.

NATH: It is wrong even to feel that way.

SEVA: Not at all. If anyone behaves in a certain way, it is
bound to produce such reactions. Who is in the
wrong—one who indulges in such behaviour, or one
who points it out? I say this is a case of getting angry
with the mountain and breaking the house. To be
frank, you are angry with him, with Arun . . .

NATH: [*Feeling exposed.*] No. Not at all. [*Lowering his
voice.*] I won't say that I was not angry at all. No, I
am not a sage or a Mahatma, but that does not mean I
should fail to respect him . . .

    [*The door bell rings.*]

JAYAPRAKASH: [*Looks through the spy-hole and in an
undertone to Seva and Nath.*] He has come. Arun. There
are two others with him.

    [*Eerie stillness.*]

NATH: [*Tense.*] Go, open the door.

    [*Seva goes in.*

    Jayaprakash goes to open the door. Arun enters with

two others. One of them belongs to Arun's dalit community. The other is an upper caste well-wisher of the dalit community. He carries a briefcase.
Arun and the other two enter, smiling at Nath with folded hands. Nath gestures to them to sit down, he is still in a state of tension. All three sit down. The two visitors sit properly, Arun spreads himself on the chair. His posture reflects uncouth manners and theatricality. Jayaprakash stands in a corner.]

NATH: [*Avoiding Arun and looking at the other two.*] Yes, what can I do for you? What brings you here?

ARUN: I told these gentlemen 'You go by yourselves, I'm not coming.' But they simply wouldn't listen. They insisted that I accompany them, and that's how I've been dragged along. I said, all right, a chance to see my in-laws, [*Turns to his friends.*] otherwise where's the time for such visits? Nowadays there's a stream of invitations saying: 'Please give a speech, may we request you to attend this dinner, a cocktail party, at least come to tea . . . ' I am a celebrated writer now. And in high society, the celebrated writer is next in demand to the pet dog. Got it? Well . . . Oh, I must make the introductions. [*To Nath.*] This is Hammeer Rao Kamle. Noted essayist of dalit literature. An excellent but neglected writer. And this is Vamanseth Nevrgaonkar. A critic of dalit literature, he spends his money in feeding dalit writers. Runs a hotel, and, he's always fresh like the samosas in that hotel. Eh, Vamanseth? . . . These gentlemen have an association— The Progressive Dalit Literature Circle. [*He winks at both.*] Nothing much of course, but it's there! Well Sir, today one of my books is being acclaimed everywhere. It is an autobiographical novel. Actually, a copy should have been presented to you first. However, I am a busy—meaning lazy—man, and so I didn't get round to it. Well, Vamanseth, have we brought a copy?

Vamanseth is my publisher. [*Vamanseth's empty laugh
indicates that he has not brought the book.*] Didn't bring
it? Never mind. [*To Nath.*] It happens. Those who are
near are always forgotten. [*To the companions.*] But our
Nath is what we call a very profound man. His wide
ranging vision does not miss anything of value. He
would surely have read my autobiography. Tell me,
Nath saheb, have you or haven't you read it?
        [*Nath nods his head reluctantly to signify that he has.*]

ARUN: [*To his friends.*] See, my guess can never go wrong.
        [*To Nath.*] What these gentlemen say is . . . they insist,
        that you should preside over the discussion of my
        autobiography. Right, Vamanseth? Well, Hammeer
        Rao? [*Both nod their heads in agreement.*] And thereby
        the meeting will gain a kind of prestige. That's what
        they think. I have nothing to say in the matter.

NATH: [*Slightly stiff.*] There was a call about this just now.

ARUN: That must be for that other discussion . . . in the
        city library. Right now my book is the talk of the
        town. These people are my special friends. [*He points to
        them.*] You have to consider their request as a special
        one. Taking your consent for granted they have already
        announced that you will chair the discussion.

NATH: [*Surprised.*] Without my consent?

ARUN: [*To both his friends.*] Here, didn't I say so—that
        Nath saheb doesn't like such things? [*To Nath.*] But
        they said Nath is a Socialist, an MLA, surely he won't
        let us down. Nath saheb simply cannot refuse; besides,
        he is also the father-in-law, . . . that's what these people
        were saying, not I . . .

NATH: As for that, you will have so many speakers, ready
        to talk about this book.

ARUN: Of course they are ready . . . like the queues at the
        movies. I am told that professors are shocked out of
        their wits by the experiences described in this book. In
        the last five decades . . . or is it ten, Vamanseth? Such

writing has not appeared in the last ten decades—so
buzz the insects in your field of criticism. It is said that
the book will get the Sahitya Akademi award. Let it
come, who cares? [*To his friends.*] What do those
bloody buggers know of life? All Maratha literature is
stuffed with the petty bourgeois outlook and with
soppy romanticism. I am the only one after the saint
poets—who else is there? [*To Nath.*] Nath saheb, they
have already printed your name in the posters and
invitations.

NATH: [*Getting annoyed.*] I am not responsible for that.

ARUN: Of course you are not responsible, but the crowds
will come with the expectation of hearing Nath saheb's
address. Am I right, Hammeer Rao? [*Hammeer Rao
nods his head in agreement.*] If you don't come, all sorts
of rumours will float . . . silly reasons will be
fabricated . . .

NATH: [*Understanding the plot.*] What reasons?

ARUN: These people will certainly give suitable
explanations. [*Winking at Vamanseth.*] 'Due to
unavoidable circumstances, Nath saheb could not', etc.,
etc. But nowadays people have become very smart.
They read too much into such situations. They make
one plus one add up to eleven. They will say that
father-in-law and son-in-law don't see eye to eye; that I
regularly torture your daughter, and more nonsense
along those lines . . . Vamanseth, don't you think so?
[*Vamanseth nods.*] What's to stop people from saying
that I got your daughter thrown out of her house?
Other gossip will have it that the rise of the son-in-law
could not be endured by the father-in-law. The rise of
the dalit son-in-law to literary heights caused heartburn
in the upper caste, socialist father-in-law.

NATH: [*Angrily.*] Nonsense. People know what I am.

ARUN: True enough. [*To his friends.*] You have made a big
mistake in putting his name down. If there's a ruckus

don't curse me! Nath saheb, I shall not press you. You are all very busy people. It's a great honour if you can give us some of your valuable time. Your connections are with the elite. Our friends here belong to a low caste, brought up on the flesh of dead animals. Eh, Hammeer Rao? Our ancestors trudged around with a load of shit on their heads. It is my great good fortune which made a fair and lovely bird from a well-to-do, high-class background, fall to my lot. [*To his friends.*] My revered mother-in-law has always been angry with me. She would have liked a fair, rich, highly educated son-in-law with his butt glued to a high office chair. But fate wrote my name instead. A poet and a writer! And dalit at that! With not even a rag to cover my hide! So Nath saheb, you say you won't preside over the meeting? . . .

NATH: [*Controlled, decisively.*] No. Don't depend on me.

ARUN: [*Getting up.*] Let's go sir, Vamanseth, Hammeer Rao, let's shop elsewhere for a chairman. Chairmen are a dime a dozen. It was a question of the level of discussion. That's why we disturbed Nath saheb in his home. Now let's go and catch a few Sarvoday professors or Marxist scholars. They will be dying to come. [*To Nath.*] These people believed you were a well-wisher of the dalit community. That you championed the cause of 'A well in every village for the dalit'. You launched a satyagrah for that cause. You deliver socialist addresses at the State Assembly. With the trumpet call of idealism, you got your daughter married to a dalit. Therefore they thought you would surely come to this discussion. [*To his friends.*] Let's go. [*He takes them to the front door. Jayaprakash is standing there.*] Hello brother-in-law, how is your Seva dal buggering getting on? [*Both friends have gone out. Arun is right next to the door.*] Goodbye! [*Goes out and shuts the door.*]

[*Nath tormented; Jayaprakash silent.*]

NATH: [*Greatly enraged.*] Scoundrel!...[*Seva has just come in from the kitchen.*] He prints my name without even asking me...he wants to blackmail me. As though I'd go down on my knees before him. As though I'd overlook my daughter's misery and shower him with superlatives. I was nauseated by his overweening arrogance. And he's the same man who wrote that autobiography. I can't believe it. Seva, he...his visit has polluted this drawing room, this house, and this day...It stinks. Seva—you know—you see—I feel like taking a bath, like cleaning myself! Clean everything! This furniture, this floor...all this...he has made them filthy, dirty, polluted! Why did I have to come into contact with a man like this? A man like this...Why?

[*Jayaprakash has been relating the happenings to Seva.*]

JAYAPRAKASH: [*Summing up.*] He left the room like a triumphant wrestler departing from the arena.

NATH: [*Passionate.*] Huh, tell him that we too have fought battles! And with adversaries a hundred times stronger than him. I will be the last person to submit to his blackmail. I come from the tradition of saints who said, 'Don't be deceived by my appearance which seems softer than wax. The strength of my convictions can shatter rocks to fragments.' Nath Devlalikar has never been under anyone's thumb, and never shall be...

[*Paces up and down in a fury. Seva is thoughtful. Jayaprakash is only a spectator.*]

SEVA: May I say something?

NATH: [*Calming down a little, though still seething with anger.*] Yes...

SEVA: You will have to go and deliver that speech.

NATH: Oh no! I'd rather die!

SEVA: First listen to me, then do what you like. Look, we are badly trapped. If we go against his wishes, it will mean more suffering for Jyoti. He will take it out on Jyoti. [*Nath wants to say something; she stops him.*] Wait, let me finish. Jyoti's condition frightens me. It is a question of her life and death. And Jyoti is our daughter. Your refusal will make him find new ways to torment her. If you don't go to the meeting, God knows what he . . . in his madness . . . will do to Jyoti . . . [*She cannot speak further.*] Therefore, you will have to go. You will have to preside over the function. You will have to praise the book, because that is the only option left to us.

[*Nath tries to speak but cannot.*]

SEVA: Don't feel hurt by my saying so, but it is you who invited all this trouble.

[*Now Nath's fortitude cracks. He feels helpless. Drained of energy, he buries himself in the sofa.*]

NATH: [*With his head dropping.*] I accept. I will go to the meeting. I will preside over it. I will praise him as much as I can.

JAYAPRAKASH: Damn! Damn! Damn!

[*He goes out in a rage, banging the door shut. Seva comes to Nath and gently places her hand on his shoulder. Her hand moves tenderly. Darkness falls.*]

* * *

Act Two

Scene Three

Same place, about 9 o'clock at night. There is no one in the drawing-room. Only a night lamp burns. The door is opened with a latchkey; Seva and Nath enter from outside. Seva switches the lights on.

Nath sits down on the sofa, dispirited and weary. Jayaprakash enters from outside; closes the door softly. Jayaprakash and Seva look at the tired, listless Nath.

A few moments pass.

SEVA: Shall I get you some water?

NATH: No.

JAYAPRAKASH: Bhai, shall I make some coffee for you?

NATH: No. It's all right.

SEVA: [*To Nath.*] Won't you lie down for sometime?

JAYAPRAKASH: Shall I press your head? It will refresh you.

NATH: Am I sick or something? Look, I'm fine. As soon as I came in, I sat down without changing my clothes. That's all.

JAYAPRAKASH: Shall I play that Ravi Shankar record you like?

NATH: Prakash, what's the matter? You are breaking all records in filial devotion today.

JAYAPRAKASH: No, I just asked.

SEVA: [*With an effort, to Nath.*] You spoke well. Prakash, don't you think so?

JAYAPRAKASH: People were saying that Bhai's speech was the most balanced, measured and to the point.

NATH: You people seem to have decided to say what you don't mean.

JAYAPRAKASH: Not at all.

NATH: Do you think I cannot hear myself speak? What I
   spoke today was rubbish, all of it. Hollow,
   hypocritical, flat and meaningless drivel!

SEVA: We liked your speech.

NATH: Seva, has it come to this that you feel you have to
   go against your nature to praise me? You know very
   well I made that speech under duress.

SEVA: You only expressed your views on that book.

NATH: The views I expressed happen to be the exact
   opposite of what I feel about that book. I hate that
   book.

SEVA: That day, after reading the book, it was you who
   were full of praise for it . . .

NATH: I was a fool then. An ignorant fool. Not any more.
   That book is not a novel, it is an autobiography. It
   depicts a real person's life. And it is the responsibility
   of the author to stick to the truth. But the book has
   not even an ounce of truth in it, it is a hoax. It is a
   crafty, sanctimonious, artistic hoax. Nothing is real in
   that book. Neither the man nor his values. At best it is
   good fiction and therefore, Seva, most dangerous.
   Because this kind of hypocrisy marks a rank
   opportunist. The devil lurks within that opportunist.
   That book is no autobiography; it is pulp fiction based
   on half truths. [*Taking a deep breath.*] No. Not all dalits
   can be like that. They know what suffering is. They
   have paid a high price to be counted as human beings.
   They understand their own sufferings, therefore they
   will certainly know the sufferings of others. [*Starts
   pacing up and down in distress. Anguish on his face.*] Did
   you see Jyoti, Seva? How thin she looked! She came
   late and sat somewhere at the back. When I saw her
   from the dais I had the urge to go up to her and say:
   'Child, what have you done to yourself?' I could read
   her face. How it reflected the hollowness of my speech!

From the time she was eleven, she has been the most relentless critic of my speech-making. As soon as I entered the house she would catch hold of me. She'd say, 'Bhai, you talked nonsense, don't do it again.' If she happened to like my speech, my child's eyes would brim with delight and pride. And that same Jyoti had heard me today . . . [*Falls silent.*] My blatant lying today will make Jyoti's life a little more tolerable, won't it, Seva?

SEVA: [*Sombre.*] You did what I asked. I don't know how I can repay you.

NATH: Do you think I did it for you? I did it for the sake of my brave and innocent daughter. What is this compared to her having ruined her whole life for my sake?

SEVA: Whatever she did, she did out of her own free will. Don't blame yourself for it unnecessarily.

NATH: No, who knows, she might have got herself out of it in time. She is impulsive but not shallow. I put our social commitments to the test. Told her 'Well done, go ahead! This is also a revolutionary method.' I closed the doors upon her return. I realize all this now.

SEVA: Nath, *she* decided to marry Arun. It was her decision. Even if you had not said anything, she would have gone ahead with the marriage.

NATH: You warned me several times. But I didn't pay any attention. I had this maniacal urge to uproot casteism and caste distinctions from our society. As a result I pushed my own daughter into a sea of misery . . .

JAYAPRAKASH: Bhai, please, is it necessary to say all these things?

NATH: Yes. There comes a time when one must re-examine one self. Even if it is a futile exercise.

SEVA: Nath, you are unnecessarily blaming yourself.

NATH: Not at all.

SEVA: As it is you are in a state of tension; and on top of that . . .

NATH: Are these vain fancies? Do you think I am so
   sentimental? Politics has given me the hide of a rhinoceros.
JAYAPRAKASH: Bhai, you sounded tired during the ceremony
   today.
NATH: You are mistaken. That was the lump which came
   to my throat when I read Arun Athavale's masterpiece.
   I deliberately managed to sound hoarse. I picked the
   most beautiful words in the language and murdered
   them as I flung them at the public. I distorted the
   words of great men and reduced them to dust. Byron
   and Kusumagraj are poets very dear to our hearts. I
   cheerfully strangled them. At one time, how deeply we
   had been influenced by Khandekar's maudlin idealism.
   Today, wherever he is, Khandekar must be turning in
   his grave. Today I used even him. Why? Why did I
   commit such sins? For the sake of my precious
   daughter, my innocent child. If she has committed any
   crime it is this: she took her father's words for gospel
   truth. She adopted her father's values. She was guided
   by her father's humanism and liberalism. Jayaprakash,
   do me a favour. Reject your father. Learn to see
   through his naïveté and idiocy. Don't ever rely on his
   wisdom. If you do, you too will ruin yourself.
SEVA: [*Interrupting.*] Don't say that! You are under severe
   strain. Come in and rest. I will sit with you. Or I will
   make dinner. You sit and talk to me.
NATH: Who stops you? Go, Prakash, go and do your
   work. You can go. I can be alone.
JAYAPRAKASH: You don't look all right Bhai . . . you look as
   if you've lost something . . .
NATH: Huh! Everything is wrong with this country, but
   the politician can never go wrong. What can he lose?
   He is the chess player. The pawns get knocked out, not
   the player.
SEVA: [*Going close to Nath and touching him.*] Come, we'll
   go in . . .

NATH: No, no. Why? I'm all right.

SEVA: [*Virtually forcing him to get up.*] Do I ever order you around? Please!

NATH: This is too much.
[*Goes in with Seva reluctantly.*
Jayaprakash is alone on the stage. He takes a book out of the shelf. Stretches out on the sofa and begins to read. The door bell rings. Jayaprakash is surprised at first. Then he opens the door. It is Jyoti at the door. Pregnant. Lean.]

JAYAPRAKASH: [*Unbelievingly.*] Jyo!
[*Jyoti comes in. Shuts the door.*]

JYOTI: Where's Bhai?

JAYAPRAKASH: He is inside. Mother is with him.

JYOTI: Why? He's not well?

JAYAPRAKASH: No, he's all right. Only somewhat disturbed. But what brings you here?

JYOTI: Nothing. Wanted to have a word with Bhai. It was difficult at the meeting, so I had to come here.

JAYAPRAKASH: So late?

JYOTI: He is not asleep already, is he?

JAYAPRAKASH: I don't know. Go and see.

JYOTI: [*Considers this.*] No. If he is not asleep, tell him I have come and would like to talk to him.

JAYAPRAKASH: [*Sensing her formality.*] If he is asleep, then? Shall I tell Ma you are here?

JYOTI: All right. But it is Bhai I have come to see.
[*Jayaprakash goes in. He has still not got over his astonishment. Jyoti remains seated, as if in a stranger's house.*
The telephone rings. Keeps ringing. Seva comes out from inside.]

SEVA: [*Looks at Jyoti from head to foot as she picks up the phone.*] Jyoti! Couldn't you come inside?
[*Jyoti doesn't answer. Seva picks up the phone.*]

SEVA: [*On the phone.*] Hello, who's speaking? Madhu? Seva

here. Bhai? He's asleep. He is a little unwell . . . no, no,
nothing to worry about, just a little . . . Shall I ask him
to call you when he gets up? All right, I'll tell him.
[*Hangs up.*]

JYOTI: [*Getting up.*] I'll see him later.

SEVA: [*Nonplussed.*] What's this, you've only just come and
you want to leave at once?

JYOTI: [*Moving towards the door.*] Tell Bhai I'll call him
before I come.

SEVA: [*In wonder.*] Jyoti! Why all this drama?

JYOTI: I had something to discuss with Bhai.

SEVA: He is coming. Where are you pushing off to? Dinner
is ready . . .

   [*Jyoti does not react. She continues to stand shrinking
   in a corner.*]

SEVA: Have dinner with us before you go, if you don't
mind . . . [*Nath comes out.*]

NATH: [*Sees Jyoti and comes towards her with great affection.*]
Jyo! You have come, my child! Why are you standing
there near the door? Come, come here. Here, sit down.
[*He leads her towards the sofa and makes her sit down.*]
What makes you come here so late? But it's wonderful
that you came. Ask Seva if you like, I was talking
about you just this minute. You as a child, the only
outspoken critic of my speech-making . . . Jyoti, let me
tell you, from the bottom of my heart I beg your
forgiveness. Today you had to listen to a lousy speech
of mine. I simply could not put any life into it. I gave
a totally bad, wretched and shameful performance
today. After such a long time you, my child, were in
the audience. A rare occasion. A precious one. But it's
my misfortune that I spoke so badly. Today I'm sure
you said to yourself: What kind of a man is he . . . my
father!

JYOTI: [*Dryly.*] I wanted to have a word with you.

NATH: And I am chattering on as usual. Force of habit.

Won't die till I am dead. Seva, is the food ready? [*To Jyoti.*] Come, let's talk at the dining table. With each mouthful I talk less. Come . . .

JYOTI: [*Coldly.*] No. We will talk here. This is the right place. [*Looks at Seva.*]

SEVA: Do you want me to leave?

JYOTI: It will be better if you do.
[*Seva goes away hurt. Nath becomes acutely aware of Jyoti's hostility.*]

NATH: Tell me.

JYOTI: [*Avoids looking at him at first. Then, suddenly faces him squarely.*] Why did you come to the meeting today?

NATH: [*Confused by the unexpectedness of the question.*] Who, me? Why, because I was invited. Didn't you see my name in the papers, and on the posters?

JYOTI: Why did you speak at the meeting?

NATH: [*Becoming uneasy.*] People like us attend meetings only to give speeches.

JYOTI: It's a lie!

NATH: Why? Why do you think it's a lie? Look here, it had been decided that I should give a speech. It was a discussion and I chaired it.

JYOTI: Why did you make a speech on Arun's book?

NATH: I was bad, I know. The speech was lousy. But I had liked the book.

jyoti: Bhai, don't lie to me. Why did you make a speech on Arun's book?

NATH: [*Deciding to lie.*] Because I found it a great book. If you like you can ask your mother about it.

JYOTI: [*Acidly.*] No. You are lying . . .

NATH: [*In a pathetic voice.*] No, no. That's not true. Look, ask Prakash . . . or call up Vasant and check it out.

JYOTI: You did not like that book.

NATH: [*Somewhat alarmed, yet with force.*] What makes you imagine that?

JYOTI: Could anyone have made a speech like that if he
         had genuinely liked it?
NATH: I am telling you, I was bad today, things wouldn't
         jell, that's all.
JYOTI: You are trying to dodge the issue. This is not the
         reason for your participation in the discussion today.
NATH: I mean yes, Arun Rao had come here . . . he must
         have told you.
JYOTI: You attended that meeting and made a speech only
         because you were afraid that if you didn't, Arun would
         torture me more.
NATH: [*Hit hard, yet continuing in the same vein.*] Well, I
         won't say that it was not one of the considerations.
JYOTI: [*In a cutting tone.*] It was the sole consideration.
         There was no other consideration. Your speech today
         was not only lousy, it was a hireling's speech. You
         attended the meeting against your wishes, you praised
         that book against your wishes.
NATH: [*Trying to explain.*] Jyoti . . .
JYOTI: I would have rather died under torture. Why did
         you make that speech? Did you have to dole out
         charity to me?
NATH: No, it wasn't charity . . . After all, we are a family.
JYOTI: No. I don't belong to this family.
NATH: You can say what you like in anger, but . . .
JYOTI: [*In a harsh voice.*] I don't belong to this family. I
         don't belong to anyone in this house. Don't ever say it
         again.
NATH: [*Trying to turn it into a joke.*] Well then, to whom
         do you belong?
JYOTI: You know very well to whom I belong. I belong to
         someone who makes your clean and pure soul impure
         by his touch.
NATH: You are wrong, Jyoti.
JYOTI: No more lies, please!
NATH: [*Caught in a trap.*] What proof do you have, to say

I don't like him? He has always been welcome in this house . . . As a poet and as a writer he has always been given due respect.

JYOTI: I heard it all in your speech hired for the occasion! In your false, deceitful speech! I know what you really wanted to say. I heard what you were unable to say. Whenever your eyes fell on him, they dripped poison. After the meeting he tried to see you, and I saw how you ignored the man you hold in such high esteem! Bhai, after today you cannot fool me. In your heart there's just hatred for Arun and nothing else.

NATH: [*In a softer tone, trying to explain.*] You are making a mistake. I don't hate Arun, I hate only those tendencies—those tendencies . . .

JYOTI: Tendencies! I grew up listening to such talk day in and day out. 'Hatred, not for the man, but for his tendencies. No man is fundamentally evil, he is good. He has certain propensities towards evil. They must be transformed. Completely uprooted and destroyed. And then, the earth will become heaven. It is essential to awaken the god slumbering within man . . .' All false, vicious claptrap! The truth is, you knew very well that man and his inherent nature are never really two different things. Both are one, and inseparable. And either you accept it in totality, or you reject it if you can. Very often you don't have a choice. Putting man's beastliness to sleep, and awakening the godhead within is an absurd notion. You made me waste twenty years of my life before I could discover this. I had to learn it on the strength of my own experience. I had to meet a man named Arun Athavale. Arun gave me what you had withheld from me. I must acknowledge my debt to him.

NATH: Look, Jyoti, this is not a matter which can be cleared up in a few words. But with a cool head, in detail . . .

JYOTI: You analyse it in detail, with a cool head. I don't

have the time, nor a cool head. I have to go and get on
with the struggle. Come and watch Arun at night when
he staggers home roaring drunk, if you have the guts.
There is a savage beast in his eyes, his lips, his
face . . . in every single limb. And bestiality is
something which cannot be separated from him. In the
beginning, like an idiot, I used to search for that Arun
who is above and beyond this beastliness, I used to call
out to him, take him in my arms. Hard experience
taught me I would always fail. Arun is both the beast,
and the lover. Arun is the demon, and also the poet.
Both are bound together, one within the other, they
are one. So closely bound that at times it is not
possible to distinguish the demon from the poet. Filthy
cursing is a part of his frenzied love; a sudden shower
of hard, ardent kisses accompanies the rain of
blows.After going through these miseries, if the broken
body finds some rest and wakes to engage itself in the
routine, then, a few lines come to hand, lines steeped
in feeling, fragments of poetry filled with the throb of
pain . . . And a fresh start is made, love springs once
again; even while the ear is defiled by plots base and
vile, to defraud and trick well-wishers . . . All these
things are done by the same person, at the same time!
Tell me, where is that beast I should drag out and
destroy, where is that god I should rouse from his
sleep? Tell me . . . Arun is made of all these things
bound together and I have to accept him as he is,
because I cannot reject him.

NATH: Why not? I will support you if it comes to that.

JYOTI: It will not happen, Bhai, because you yourself have
taught us that one must not turn one's back upon the
battlefield. It was you who always taught us that it is
cowardly to bow down to circumstances. It was you
who constantly intoned those phrases which never
failed to get the audience cheering. And we also

clapped, and said 'Our father is a great man.' You
taught us those poems which said: 'I march with utter
faith in the goal'; 'I grow with rising hopes' and
'Cowards stay ashore, every wave opens a path for me.'
It was you who made us learn these lines. And scores
of poems like them. This drug, Bhai, has entered and
mingled with our blood. The poison has numbed our
entire consciousness. We cannot run away. To save
one's self by running away may be the smart thing to
do, and other people may get away with this kind of
cleverness, but even if running away was the general
rule of conduct, *we* shall continue to recite 'March on,
Oh soldier!' and continue to lose our lives as guinea
pigs in the experiment, and you, Bhai . . . you will go
on safely rousing the god sleeping in man.

NATH: [*In pain.*] Jyoti, don't say that . . .

JYOTI: This is the truth. To whom can I speak this truth
but to you? That's why I came. [*Getting up.*] I'm going.

NATH: Wait, Jyoti. Please don't go away like this . . . Let's
give some more thought to it.

JYOTI: You think about it, I have to stop thinking and
learn to live. I think a lot. Suffer a lot. Not from the
blows, but from my thoughts, I can't bear them much
longer . . . forgive me, Bhai, I said things I shouldn't
have. But I couldn't help it. I was deeply offended by
your hypocrisy. I thought: why did this man have to
inject and drug us everyday with truth and goodness?
And if he can get away from it at will, what right had
he to close all our options? I haven't been able to
forget an image I saw years ago on my way to school.
A man opened the lids of two baskets slung upon the
pole he carried. On his shoulder. And from them, two
shaking, swaying, staggering creatures slipped out,
human in appearance, their wrinkled skin covering
twisted bodies. Someone said these people kidnap little
children, break their limbs and make them cripples.

Bhai, forgive me for my words, but you have made us . . . [*She cannot go on.*]

    [*Nath is stunned. Jyoti moves towards the door.*]

NATH: [*In a pathetic tone.*] You will come again, won't you, Jyoti?

JYOTI: [*With certitude.*] No. When I come here I begin to hate my world. I want to ignore that truth which I have come to perceive, though rather late in life. I want to become blind once again. Hereafter I have to live in that world, which is mine . . . [*Pausing.*] and die there. Say sorry to Ma. Tell her none of you should come to my house . . . this is my order.

NATH: Your delivery . . .

JYOTI: [*Harshly.*] I have my husband. I am not a widow. Even if I become one I shan't knock at your door. I am not Jyoti Yadunath Devlalikar now, I am Jyoti Arun Athavale, a scavenger. I don't say harijan. I despise the term. I am an untouchable, a scavenger. I am one of them. Don't touch me. Fly from my shadow, otherwise my fire will scorch your comfortable values.

    [*Jyoti goes away. The latch clicks as the door bangs shut. Drained of life, Nath looks in the direction of Jyoti's exit. Background score rising to fury. Spreads. Sounds of huge buildings hurtling down.*

Spotlight on Nath's face fades and he staggers in search of light. The crashing of buildings gets louder. The sound inspires a deep dread.

The light that Nath manages to reach goes out. He moves towards the faint lights which are still on. He stands still. The light comes and goes.

Nath breaks down and buries himself in the sofa. He shrinks into it. The crashes continue and the terror mounts to a fever pitch.]

CURTAIN

* * *

Afterword

Vijay Tendulkar was awarded the Saraswati Samman for this play. What follows is excerpted from his speech at the awards ceremony. The extract throws some light on the ideas governing the play.

The work which has been selected for the Saraswati Samman is not the story of a victory; it is the admission of defeat and intellectual confusion. It gives expression to a deep-rooted malaise and its pains.

Victory and fame are normally honoured. The ambition of those who jump into the fray with the aim of winning is honoured. That is why this award leaves me disturbed and confused. I am wondering what I have really done to deserve it.

I have written about my own experiences and about what I have seen in others around me. I have been true to all this and have not cheated my generation. I did not attempt to simplify matters and issues for the audience when presenting my plays, though that would have been the easier option. Sometimes my plays jolted society out of its stupor and I was punished. I faced this without regrets. It is an old habit with me to do what I am told not to do. My plays could not have been about anything else. They contain my perception of society and its values and I cannot write what I do not perceive.

You are honouring me with the Saraswati Samman today for a play for which I once had a slipper hurled at me. Perhaps it is the fate of the play to have earned both this honour and that insult. As its creator, I respect both verdicts.